THE SHIFTING LANDSCAPE OF TECH CAREERS

ONESIMUS MALATJI

The Shifting Landscape Of Tech Careers

By: Onesimus Malatji

Fair Use Notice:

This book may contain copyrighted material used for educational and illustrative purposes. Such material is used under the "fair use" provisions of copyright law.

Third-Party Content:

This book may reference or include content from third-party sources. The author and publisher do not endorse or take responsibility for the accuracy or content of such third-party material.

Endorsements:

Any endorsement, testimonial, or representation contained in this book reflects the author's personal views and opinions. It does not imply an endorsement by any third party.
Results Disclaimer: The success stories and examples mentioned in this book are not guarantees of individual success. Actual results may vary based on various factors, including effort and circumstances.

Results Disclaimer:

The success stories and examples mentioned in this book are not guarantees of individual success. Actual results may vary based on various factors, including effort and circumstances.
No Guarantee of Outcome: The strategies, techniques, and advice provided in this book are based on the author's experiences and research. However, there is no guarantee that following these strategies will lead to a specific outcome or result.

Fair Use Notice:

This book may contain copyrighted material used for educational and illustrative purposes. Such material is used under the "fair use" provisions of copyright law.

DEDICATION

Being one of the difficulties in my family, always stubborn, I thank God I turned out alright. I dedicate this book to my mother, Esther Malatji. I will always love you. You have raised me well until I became a fully grown man. Thank you for your prayers and support during my tough times in life. Additionally, I extend my heartfelt dedication to my beautiful wife, the partner of my life, Petunia. You have been there for me and our family, and you are truly one in a million – the best motivator. I thank God for having you as my spouse, partner, and my inspiration; you are one of my most special and wonderful gifts. During times of trials, you have never walked out on us. Thank you. I love you so much.

I also send this dedication to my brother Edward "Gong," one of the greatest creative businesspersons alive. Thank you for being a wonderful brother and supporting me in times of need and trial. May God bless you and increase your business anointing. I love you so much. Special greetings to my sister Bertha, your passion for food will undoubtedly touch the world. I love you.

Furthermore, I extend my love and dedication to my brother Mohau; I will always cherish you, brother. Special Dedication for Galetsang & Dineo I will always love you no matter what. This is also for my friends, and fellow soldiers in war: Zama, Panana, Fina, Tshwane, Blessing, Lowen, Neo, I love you guys – you are my family. Special Gratitude to my inspirer my mother. I deeply respect the gift that God has put in you, and I am immensely grateful for having you while I was putting this book together.
Thank you, my dear mother, Esther Malatji. I love you so much

ACKNOWLEDGMENTS

I extend my deepest gratitude to everyone who has been a part of this incredible journey, both seen and unseen. Your support, encouragement, and unwavering belief in me have been the driving force behind the creation of this book.

To my family, for standing by me through thick and thin, for believing in my dreams, and for being a constant source of inspiration – your love and encouragement have been my guiding light.

To my friends, mentors, and colleagues, your valuable insights and feedback have shaped the ideas within these pages. Your willingness to share your wisdom and experiences has enriched this work beyond measure.

To all those who have supported me on my path, whether through a kind word, a helping hand, or a moment of shared understanding, thank you. Your presence in my life has made all the difference.

To the countless individuals who have faced challenges and setbacks, yet continued to strive for greatness, your stories have fueled the inspiration behind these words. May you find solace and encouragement within these pages.

And finally, to the readers who have embarked on this journey with me, thank you for allowing me to share my thoughts and experiences. It is my hope that this book serves as a beacon of hope, a source of guidance, and a reminder that fulfillment can be found in every step of life's intricate tapestry.

With heartfelt appreciation,

Onesimus Malatji

THE SHIFTING LANDSCAPE OF TECH CAREERS

TABLE OF CONTECT   **PAGES**

THE SHIFTING LANDSCAPE OF TECH CAREERS

DEFINING THE FOURTH INDUSTRIAL REVOLUTION

In the grand tapestry of human history, industrial revolutions have acted as pivotal turning points, reshaping societies, economies, and the very fabric of our existence. From the advent of mechanized factories in the 18th century to the rise of the internet in the 20th century, these revolutions have been marked by transformative technological advances. Today, we stand on the cusp of the Fourth Industrial Revolution, a period that promises to eclipse its predecessors in terms of the scope and scale of change it brings.

A Historical Perspective

Before delving into the specifics of the Fourth Industrial Revolution, it's essential to take a step back and briefly revisit its predecessors. The First Industrial Revolution, characterized by the mechanization of production, ushered in the era of steam engines and textile machinery. The Second Industrial Revolution was the age of electricity and the telegraph, marking the dawn of mass production. The Third Industrial Revolution, often referred to as the Digital Revolution, brought about the rise of computers and the internet, fundamentally altering the way information was processed and shared.

The Fourth Industrial Revolution: An Evolution of Connectivity and Intelligence

So, what sets the Fourth Industrial Revolution apart? At its core, this revolution is about the convergence of digital, physical, and biological realms. It's a fusion of advances in artificial intelligence, the Internet of Things (IoT), blockchain, quantum computing, 5G technology, and biotechnology. The Fourth Industrial Revolution is marked by an unprecedented level of connectivity and intelligence, where machines can not only process vast amounts of data but also make sense of it, learn from it, and interact with the physical world in ways previously unimaginable.

Key Technologies of the Fourth Industrial Revolution

1. **Artificial Intelligence and Machine Learning:** AI systems can learn from data and make decisions, creating the potential for autonomous machines and intelligent automation.

2. **The Internet of Things (IoT):** The interconnectivity of devices, sensors, and systems allows for real-time data exchange and smarter decision-making in various applications.

3. **Blockchain and Decentralization:** Blockchain technology provides secure and transparent ways of recording transactions, fostering trust and enabling new forms of digital collaboration.

4. **Quantum Computing:** Quantum computers have the potential to solve complex problems that are currently intractable for classical computers, impacting fields like cryptography, materials science, and optimization.

5. **5G Technology:** 5G networks enable faster, more reliable communication and pave the way for advancements in augmented and virtual reality, remote surgery, and smart cities.

6. **Biotechnology and Genetic Engineering:** Advances in biotechnology are revolutionizing healthcare, agriculture, and environmental sustainability through gene editing and personalized medicine.

The Pervasiveness of the Fourth Industrial Revolution

What distinguishes this revolution is the breadth of its impact. It transcends individual industries, touching everything from manufacturing and healthcare to finance, transportation, and entertainment. Its influence is not limited to the corporate world; it extends to the very way we live, work, and connect with one another. The Fourth Industrial Revolution is altering the landscape of the global economy and challenging traditional models of business and governance.

ARTIFICIAL INTELLIGENCE AND MACHINE LEARNING

In the realm of technology, few terms have garnered as much attention and fascination as "Artificial Intelligence" (AI). Its implications are far-reaching, touching every aspect of our lives, from how we work and communicate to how we access information and even how we make decisions. Central to the Fourth Industrial Revolution, AI, and its subset, Machine Learning, are transforming industries and reshaping the world in profound ways.

Understanding Artificial Intelligence

At its core, Artificial Intelligence refers to the creation of computer systems that can perform tasks that typically require human intelligence. These tasks encompass a broad spectrum, ranging from problem-solving and decision-making to natural language understanding and image recognition. The development of AI systems involves simulating human thought processes, often using algorithms and vast amounts of data.

Machine Learning: The Heart of AI

Machine Learning (ML) is a subset of AI that has gained immense prominence. It's the practice of developing algorithms that enable computer systems to learn from data, improving their performance over time without explicit programming. In essence, machine learning algorithms discover patterns, make predictions, and continuously adapt as they process more information.

AI and Machine Learning in Practice

The real-world applications of AI and Machine Learning are extensive, and their influence is felt across various sectors:

1. **Autonomous Vehicles:** Self-driving cars rely on AI and ML to interpret data from sensors and make real-time decisions to navigate safely.

2. **Healthcare:** AI algorithms can analyse medical data to assist in diagnosing diseases and recommend treatment plans.

3. **E-commerce:** Recommendation systems powered by ML algorithms personalize product suggestions based on a user's preferences and behaviors.

4. **Finance:** Fraud detection and algorithmic trading are driven by AI's capacity to analyse vast datasets and detect anomalies.

5. **Natural Language Processing (NLP):** Virtual assistants like Siri and chatbots that engage in human-like conversations are driven by NLP and machine learning.

6. **Image and Speech Recognition:** ML algorithms enable image and speech recognition systems, powering everything from facial recognition technology to voice-activated assistants.

Challenges and Ethical Considerations

As AI and ML continue to advance, they raise several challenges and ethical considerations. These include:

1. **Bias and Fairness:** AI systems can inherit biases from training data, leading to unfair or discriminatory outcomes.

2. **Privacy and Security:** The collection of vast amounts of data for AI can pose privacy and security risks if not adequately managed.

3. **Transparency and Accountability:** The opacity of AI decision-making can be problematic, especially when it's used in critical areas like healthcare or law enforcement.

The Future of AI and Machine Learning

The journey of AI and Machine Learning is far from over. As technology continues to evolve, the future holds the promise of even more sophisticated AI systems, including those capable of deep learning, advanced natural language understanding, and more. The impact of these technologies will continue to reverberate through industries, from healthcare and finance to transportation and entertainment.

IMPACTS ON INDUSTRIES

The Fourth Industrial Revolution, driven by advanced technologies such as artificial intelligence, machine learning, the Internet of Things, and blockchain, is creating seismic shifts in various industries. These technologies are reshaping traditional business models, processes, and customer experiences across a wide spectrum of sectors.

Manufacturing: Smarter and More Efficient Production

Automation and data analytics are optimizing production in the manufacturing sector. Smart factories are becoming the norm, reducing downtime and enhancing product quality. Predictive maintenance is now possible, minimizing costly equipment failures. Additionally, 3D printing is revolutionizing the prototyping and production of customized components.

Healthcare: Revolutionizing Patient Care

The healthcare industry is leveraging data-driven insights and AI to improve patient care. Electronic health records enable real-time access to patient data, while AI-powered diagnostic tools can aid in early disease detection. Telemedicine is on the rise, offering remote healthcare services, and robotic surgery is improving the precision of medical procedures.

Finance: Fintech and Digital Transformation

The financial sector is undergoing significant changes. Fintech companies are disrupting traditional banking and financial services by offering innovative solutions, including digital payments, peer-to-peer lending, and robot-advisors. Blockchain is transforming the way financial transactions are conducted, improving transparency and security.

Transportation: The Road to Autonomous Mobility

Transportation is on the brink of transformation with autonomous vehicles. Self-driving cars and trucks promise to increase safety and efficiency on the roads. Electric vehicles are becoming more prevalent, contributing to reduced carbon emissions. Ride-sharing and mobility-as-a-service platforms are changing the way people think about transportation.

Education: E-Learning and Personalized Learning

The Fourth Industrial Revolution is reshaping education. E-learning platforms and digital resources are making education more accessible. Personalized learning powered by AI adapts to individual student needs. Virtual and augmented reality are enhancing the educational experience.

Entertainment: Immersive Experiences and Digital Content

The entertainment industry is embracing immersive experiences with augmented and virtual reality. Streaming services are dominating the distribution of digital content, while AI algorithms recommend personalized entertainment options. Gaming has seen a significant shift towards cloud-based gaming and augmented reality gaming experiences.

Energy: Smart Grids and Sustainable Solutions

The energy sector is adopting smart grid technology to enhance efficiency and reliability. Renewable energy sources such as solar and wind power are being integrated into existing grids. Battery storage and energy management systems are helping consumers reduce their carbon footprint.

Agriculture: Precision Farming and Sustainability

Agriculture is undergoing a revolution with precision farming techniques. Drones and sensors enable farmers to monitor crops, conserve water, and reduce the use of chemicals. Blockchain is being used to track the origin and safety of food products.

Retail: Personalized Shopping Experiences

In the retail sector, AI-driven recommendations and chatbots provide personalized shopping experiences. E-commerce is on the rise, and brick-and-mortar stores are incorporating technology to offer seamless in-store and online shopping experiences.

These are just a few examples of how the Fourth Industrial Revolution is reshaping industries. As we explore these impacts, you'll gain insights into the evolving career opportunities and challenges within each sector. Whether you're looking to start a new career or adapt your existing one, understanding these industry shifts is essential for navigating the dynamic landscape of the Fourth Industrial Revolution.

SOCIETAL TRANSFORMATIONS

The Fourth Industrial Revolution isn't just reshaping industries and the way we work; it's also profoundly influencing the structure of societies, our values, and the way we interact with one another. From the digital transformation of daily life to changes in how we govern and educate, the impacts of this revolution are far-reaching.

Digital Transformation

The Fourth Industrial Revolution is synonymous with the digital transformation of our society. Digital technologies have altered how we communicate, connect, and even perceive the world around us. Smartphones, social media, and the Internet of Things have become integral parts of our daily lives.

Privacy and Data Security

The pervasive use of technology has raised critical questions about privacy and data security. With the collection of vast amounts of personal data, individuals and organizations must navigate the complex landscape of data protection, privacy laws, and ethical considerations.

Workforce Changes and the Gig Economy

The traditional employment model is evolving. The Fourth Industrial Revolution has given rise to the gig economy, where individuals work on a project-by-project basis. This new work paradigm offers flexibility and independence but also brings challenges related to job security, benefits, and income stability.

Sustainability and Environmental Tech

As societies become increasingly aware of environmental concerns, there's a growing emphasis on sustainability. Environmental tech, including renewable energy, green transportation, and waste reduction solutions, is playing a pivotal role in mitigating the environmental impact of industrial activities.

Healthcare Revolution

The Fourth Industrial Revolution is reshaping healthcare by introducing telemedicine, wearable health tech, and personalized medicine. Patients can access healthcare services remotely, while AI and big data analytics assist in diagnosing and treating diseases.

Technological Inclusivity and Accessibility

Efforts are being made to ensure that the benefits of the Fourth Industrial Revolution are inclusive. This involves addressing the digital divide, providing technological access to underserved communities, and creating accessible technologies for people with disabilities.

Educational Transformation

The education sector is experiencing significant changes. E-learning platforms are providing access to education from anywhere in the world. Personalized learning is catering to individual student needs, and the integration of technology is reshaping the classroom experience.

Technological Inclusion and Accessibility

The concept of "digital citizenship" is emerging as societies grapple with the challenges of technology. Ensuring equal access to technology, promoting digital literacy, and addressing issues related to online safety and ethics are critical aspects of this transformation.

The Age of Hyperconnectivity

Societies are becoming increasingly interconnected, thanks to advancements in communication technology. Social media, virtual reality, and online collaboration tools are changing how we connect, share information, and build communities.

Challenges and Ethical Considerations

With these societal transformations come complex challenges and ethical considerations. These include issues related to data privacy, cybersecurity, equitable access to technology, and the social implications of automation and AI.

Conclusion

Societal transformations driven by the Fourth Industrial Revolution are altering the way we live, work, and relate to one another. The impact of these changes is far-reaching, with both opportunities and challenges. As we continue to explore the dynamic landscape of the Fourth Industrial Revolution, it's essential to recognize the societal shifts and be proactive in adapting to this ever-evolving world. Understanding these transformations is crucial for anyone seeking to navigate the opportunities and challenges of the Fourth Industrial Revolution effectively.

CHALLENGES AND ETHICAL CONSIDERATIONS

The Fourth Industrial Revolution brings about transformative technologies that hold the promise of improving our lives, but they also present a range of complex challenges and ethical dilemmas. It's essential to navigate this revolution with a keen awareness of these issues.

Job Displacement and Economic Inequality

Job Displacement: As automation and AI advance, there is a concern that some jobs may become obsolete, leading to job displacement. Workers in industries heavily impacted by automation may face the challenge of reskilling or transitioning to new roles.

Economic Inequality: The wealth generated by this technological revolution is not evenly distributed. Economic inequality can widen as those with the right skills benefit disproportionately, while others are left behind. Ethical considerations revolve around ensuring that the benefits of the revolution are more equitably distributed.

Bias in Artificial Intelligence

AI systems are only as unbiased as the data they are trained on. Biases present in historical data can perpetuate unfair and discriminatory outcomes. Addressing these biases and ensuring that AI technologies are equitable is a pressing ethical challenge.

Data Privacy and Security

The collection and use of vast amounts of data in the Fourth Industrial Revolution raise questions about individual privacy and data security. It is essential to strike a balance between data-driven innovation and safeguarding personal information.

Loss of Human Control in Autonomous Systems

Autonomous vehicles, robots, and AI systems operate with varying degrees of autonomy. The challenge lies in determining how much autonomy is appropriate and ensuring that humans can retain control when needed. The ethical considerations pertain to accountability and responsibility when autonomous systems make decisions.

Environmental Sustainability

The environmental impact of advanced technologies is a critical concern. It is essential to develop and adopt sustainable practices, from clean energy sources to reducing e-waste. The Fourth Industrial Revolution offers opportunities to mitigate environmental challenges, but it also has the potential to exacerbate them.

Ethical AI and Robotics

As AI and robotics become more integrated into society, questions of ethics arise. What moral responsibilities do these systems have, and how do we ensure ethical behavior? This includes the ethical use of AI in fields like healthcare, criminal justice, and finance.

Transparency and Accountability

The opaqueness of AI decision-making presents ethical challenges. Understanding how AI systems arrive at conclusions is essential for transparency and accountability. If an AI system makes a decision with far-reaching consequences, who bears the responsibility if it goes wrong?

Job Redesign and Reskilling

Addressing the challenge of job displacement due to automation involves job redesign and reskilling. Ethical considerations encompass supporting individuals in their transition to new roles and ensuring that everyone has access to educational resources and opportunities.

Safeguarding Digital Identities

As digital technologies become more ingrained in our lives, safeguarding digital identities is paramount. This includes protecting against identity theft, cyberattacks, and ensuring the security of personal information.

Conclusion

The challenges and ethical considerations surrounding the Fourth Industrial Revolution are complex and multifaceted. As we navigate this transformative era, it's imperative to confront these challenges head-on while embracing the ethical imperatives of equity, transparency, accountability, and sustainability. By addressing these concerns proactively, we can work towards harnessing the full potential of the Fourth Industrial Revolution in a responsible and inclusive manner. This requires both individuals and society at large to consider the broader implications of these technologies and adopt a forward-thinking, ethical approach.

PREPARING FOR THE FUTURE

In the midst of the Fourth Industrial Revolution, preparing for the future is not just a matter of chance; it's a proactive and intentional journey. To thrive in a world of rapid technological change, individuals and organizations must embrace lifelong learning, adaptability, and foresight.

The Importance of Lifelong Learning

1. **Embracing Continuous Learning:** The pace of technological change requires a mindset of continuous learning. Skills that are relevant today may become obsolete tomorrow. Lifelong learning is the key to staying updated and relevant.

2. **Online Learning Platforms:** With the proliferation of online courses and educational resources, learning is more accessible than ever. Platforms like Coursera, edX, and Khan Academy provide a wealth of knowledge at your fingertips.

3. **Microlearning:** Short, focused learning modules can fit into busy schedules. Microlearning allows individuals to acquire new skills and knowledge in bite-sized portions.

Skills for the Future

1. **Critical Thinking:** The ability to analyse information, think critically, and make informed decisions is invaluable. In a world where data is abundant, the skill of discernment becomes paramount.

2. **Adaptability:** Being able to pivot and adapt to new technologies and changing circumstances is a vital skill. It means being open to change and ready to embrace new opportunities.

3. **Emotional Intelligence:** In an increasingly automated world, emotional intelligence, which includes empathy and understanding human emotions, becomes a crucial skill in areas such as customer service and team collaboration.

The Role of Mentoring

1. **Mentorship:** Mentorship provides guidance and support for personal and professional growth. A mentor can offer insights, share experiences, and provide a roadmap for success in your chosen field.

2. **Peer Learning:** Learning from peers who share similar experiences and challenges can be equally valuable. Peer networks can provide feedback, encouragement, and collaborative opportunities.

3. **Networking and Building Your Personal Brand**

4. **Networking:** Building a professional network is an essential part of career development. It can open doors to opportunities, provide access to valuable resources, and offer support.

5. **Personal Branding:** Cultivating a strong personal brand is essential. This includes showcasing your skills, experience, and values in a way that distinguishes you in your field.

Embracing Technological Change

1. **Tech-Savviness:** Staying informed about emerging technologies is essential. Familiarize yourself with AI, cloud computing, blockchain, and other key technologies shaping the Fourth Industrial Revolution.

2. **Experimentation:** Don't be afraid to experiment with new technologies. Hands-on experience is a valuable teacher.

Balancing Work and Life

1. **Work-Life Balance:** In a world where technology enables constant connectivity, finding a balance between work and personal life is crucial for well-being.

2. **Burnout Prevention:** Recognize the signs of burnout and implement strategies to maintain mental and emotional health.

Giving Back and Ethical Considerations

1. **Corporate Social Responsibility:** Consider the ethical impact of your work. Many organizations are embracing corporate social responsibility by contributing positively to society and the environment.

2. **Tech for Good:** Explore opportunities to leverage technology for social and environmental good. Tech for good initiatives is becoming increasingly prevalent.

Conclusion

Preparing for the future in the Fourth Industrial Revolution requires a proactive approach. Embrace lifelong learning, cultivate the skills necessary for the future, build a strong professional network, and stay open to the transformative power of technology. By combining adaptability with a strong ethical compass, you can navigate the dynamic landscape of the future with confidence and purpose. The opportunities are vast, and the key to unlocking them lies in your dedication to growth and your readiness to embrace change.

CONCLUSION

The Fourth Industrial Revolution has ushered in a world of unprecedented technological advancement, redefining industries, reshaping societies, and revolutionizing the nature of work. As we conclude this journey through the shifting landscape of tech careers, it's crucial to reflect on the insights gained and the path forward.

The Endless Potential of Tech Careers

In the Fourth Industrial Revolution, the potential for tech careers is limitless. Whether you're drawn to artificial intelligence, blockchain, cloud computing, or any other cutting-edge technology, the opportunities to make an impact are vast.

A World of Constant Change

This revolution comes with both promise and challenge. The promise lies in the ability to solve complex problems, improve lives, and create a more connected and sustainable world. The challenge is to keep pace with rapid technological change and navigate the ethical considerations that arise along the way.

The Power of Adaptability and Lifelong Learning

Adaptability and lifelong learning are the linchpins of success in this dynamic era. Embracing change and fostering the ability to pivot and acquire new skills will be your greatest assets in a world of constant innovation.

Embracing Ethical Technology

As we venture into the future, it's crucial to remember the importance of ethics and responsibility. Ethical considerations extend to how we use technology, the impact it has on individuals and societies, and the responsibility we hold as creators and consumers of technology.

Community, Support, and Mentorship

Navigating the Fourth Industrial Revolution can be challenging, but you're not alone. Building a community of like-minded individuals, seeking mentorship, and offering support to others can make the journey more enriching and fulfilling.

Looking Ahead to an Exciting Future

The future is filled with opportunities and challenges. As you embark on your tech career journey, remember that the knowledge and skills you've gained in this book are just the beginning. Stay curious, stay adaptable, and continue learning. The tech landscape will evolve, and you have the power to shape it.

Your Journey to a Future-Ready Tech Career

Your journey to a future-ready tech career is a voyage into uncharted waters, where each day brings new possibilities and new horizons. This is a journey that requires resilience, adaptability, and a willingness to embrace change.

In the ever-shifting landscape of tech careers, one thing is certain: you have the ability to make a difference, to contribute to the ongoing transformation of our world, and to shape the future. So, take the knowledge you've gained, the insights you've gathered, and the skills you've honed, and embark on your path to a future-ready tech career with confidence and enthusiasm.

The Fourth Industrial Revolution is a chapter in human history that's still being written, and you have a role to play. Embrace the opportunities, tackle the challenges, and, most importantly, never stop learning, never stop growing, and never stop innovating. The future is yours to shape.

INTRODUCTION: THE IMPACT OF AUTOMATION ON TRADITIONAL JOBS

The world is experiencing a profound transformation, one that is being driven by the relentless march of technology. We stand at the precipice of a revolution that will redefine the very nature of work, challenge the stability of traditional job roles, and prompt us to rethink the skills and expertise required for the future.

This revolution, often referred to as the Fourth Industrial Revolution, is characterized by the convergence of digital technologies, artificial intelligence, machine learning, and automation. As we journey through this chapter, we will explore the profound implications of this convergence on what were once considered stable and unshakable traditional jobs.

For generations, certain job roles seemed impervious to the winds of change. From manufacturing and service industries to office administration and creative professions, the stability of these roles offered a sense of security. However, the rapid advancement of automation technologies has set forth a wave of disruption that is not just transforming these roles but, in some cases, rendering them obsolete.

In the pages that follow, we will delve into the heart of this transformation, examining the impact of automation on traditional jobs across various sectors. We will explore how tasks once performed by human hands are now being executed by machines, algorithms, and robots. We will scrutinize the consequences of this shift, from potential job displacement to the emergence of new roles and opportunities.

The impact of automation extends far beyond the realm of employment statistics. It encompasses the very essence of how we perceive work, the skills we value, and the ethical considerations of a world in which machines take on tasks that were once the exclusive domain of humans.

As we explore the technological forces at play and the societal implications they carry, it is crucial to understand that this chapter is not a eulogy for traditional jobs, nor is it a lament for their loss. Rather, it is a journey through the complex tapestry of change, a quest to uncover how we can adapt, re-skill, and re-imagine the world of work in a landscape shaped by automation.

So, join us on this exploration of "The Impact of Automation on Traditional Jobs," as we dissect the seismic shifts taking place in industries and the lives of those who have traditionally found their livelihoods in these roles. Together, we will discover not just the challenges, but the opportunities that this revolution holds, and how to navigate them with resilience, adaptability, and foresight.

THE AUTOMATION WAVE

As we dive deeper into the impact of automation on traditional jobs, it's essential to understand the forces behind this transformation. The "Automation Wave" is a term that encapsulates the sweeping changes driven by advanced technologies and their effects on the workforce.

The Rise of Automation Technologies

The Automation Wave is, in many ways, the culmination of years of technological advancement. It's characterized by the proliferation of several key technologies, each contributing to the transformation of traditional job roles:

1. **Artificial Intelligence (AI):** AI systems, powered by machine learning and deep learning algorithms, can perform tasks that typically require human intelligence. From natural language understanding to image recognition, AI is at the forefront of automation.

2. **Robotics:** Robots, both physical and virtual, are taking on a range of tasks across industries. From manufacturing robots that assemble products to chatbots handling customer service inquiries, robotics are redefining work processes.

3. **Machine Learning:** Machine learning algorithms can analyse data, learn from it, and make predictions or decisions without being explicitly programmed. This capability is revolutionizing data-intensive tasks in sectors such as finance, healthcare, and e-commerce.

4. **The Internet of Things (IoT):** The vast network of interconnected devices in the IoT enables real-time data exchange. This connectivity is a foundation for automation, allowing for predictive maintenance in manufacturing, smart homes, and more.

5. **Automation Software:** RPA (Robotic Process Automation) software is automating repetitive, rule-based tasks, often found in administrative and back-office functions. This form of automation is streamlining business processes.

6. **Advanced Analytics:** Advanced data analytics and big data technologies are providing organizations with insights that fuel automation. Data-driven decision-making is shaping operations in various sectors.

Industries Reshaped by Automation

The Automation Wave is not limited to a single industry; it encompasses a broad spectrum. Here are a few examples of how automation is transforming different sectors:

Manufacturing: Automation has revolutionized production lines, enabling more precise and efficient manufacturing processes. Robots are increasingly responsible for tasks ranging from assembly to quality control.

1. **Retail:** Automation is redefining customer experiences, with self-checkout kiosks and automated inventory management systems. In e-commerce, automation algorithms optimize product recommendations and logistics.

2. **Healthcare:** From robotic surgery to AI-driven diagnostics, healthcare is benefiting from automation technologies that enhance patient care, streamline administrative tasks, and advance medical research.

3. **Finance:** Fintech companies are automating various financial services, from algorithmic trading to robot-advisors. Automation is driving efficiency and transforming the customer banking experience.

4. **Transportation:** Autonomous vehicles are at the forefront of the transportation industry's transformation. Self-driving cars and drones are changing the way we move people and goods.

5. **Agriculture:** Automation in agriculture includes autonomous tractors, drones for crop monitoring, and robotic pickers. These technologies are increasing productivity and sustainability.

Job Displacement and the Changing Nature of Work

As the Automation Wave gains momentum, the impact on traditional jobs is palpable. Tasks that were once performed by humans are now being executed by machines, algorithms, and robots. The consequence is job displacement, a phenomenon that raises questions about the future of work.

The changing nature of work is not limited to job loss; it extends to job transformation. Traditional job roles are evolving, requiring a new set of skills and adaptability to automation. The key to navigating this transformation is to embrace lifelong learning, acquire digital literacy, and adapt to emerging roles in the age of automation.

AUTOMATION IN THE SERVICE INDUSTRY

The service industry, encompassing a wide array of sectors including retail, hospitality, customer service, and more, has been profoundly impacted by the Automation Wave. Automation technologies have infiltrated service-related tasks, reshaping how businesses interact with customers and conduct their operations.

1. Retail Automation

1.1. **Retail Automation:** Retail businesses are harnessing automation technologies to streamline their operations and enhance customer experiences.

1.2. **Self-Checkout Kiosks:** Automated self-checkout kiosks have become a common sight in supermarkets and stores. Customers can scan and pay for their items without cashier assistance.

1.3. **Inventory Management:** Automation software tracks inventory levels in real time, optimizing restocking processes and reducing instances of stockouts or overstock.

1.4. **Chatbots and Virtual Assistants:** Many retailers use chatbots or virtual assistants to provide customer support, answer common queries, and guide customers in their online shopping journeys.

1.5. **Personalized Recommendations:** Algorithms powered by AI analyse customer data to provide personalized product recommendations. This enhances customer engagement and boosts sales.

2. Hospitality and Tourism Automation

2.1. **Hospitality Automation:** In the hospitality and tourism sector, automation is transforming the guest experience and improving operational efficiency.

2.2. **Automated Check-In and Check-Out:** Hotels and accommodations have introduced self-service kiosks for guests to check in and out quickly. This reduces waiting times and enhances the guest experience.

2.3. **Room Service Robots:** Some hotels employ robots to deliver room service, such as food and amenities, to guest rooms.

2.4. **Online Booking and Reservation Systems:** Automation has simplified the process of booking accommodations, flights, and activities, making it convenient for travellers.

2.5. **Customer Support Chatbots:** Hospitality companies use chatbots to assist guests with inquiries and bookings, providing efficient and timely responses.

3. Customer Service and Call Centres

3.1. **Customer Service Automation:** Call centres and customer service departments have seen significant automation of routine tasks.

3.2. **Interactive Voice Response (IVR):** IVR systems use automation to route calls, gather information from callers, and provide automated responses or actions for common queries.

3.3. **Chatbots and Virtual Agents:** Customer service chatbots handle a range of inquiries, providing quick answers and freeing up human agents to address more complex issues.

3.4. **Email Automation:** Automated email responses and categorization help manage the high volume of customer emails efficiently.

4. Food Service Automation

4.1. **Food Service Automation:** Automation has found its way into food service establishments, revolutionizing how orders are placed, prepared, and delivered.

4.2. **Self-Service Kiosks:** Fast food and quick-service restaurants often use self-service kiosks, allowing customers to customize and place their orders without human intervention.

4.3. **Kitchen Automation:** In the kitchen, automation systems are employed to optimize cooking times, monitor food quality, and ensure consistency in dishes.

4.4. **Delivery Drones and Robots:** In some areas, food delivery services utilize drones and robots for efficient and contactless deliveries.

The Impact on Jobs and Workers

The integration of automation technologies in the service industry has undoubtedly streamlined processes, improved efficiency, and enhanced customer experiences. However, it has also raised concerns about job displacement.

Traditional roles in retail, hospitality, and customer service are undergoing transformation. The focus is shifting from routine, repetitive tasks to more complex, interpersonal, and value-added activities. This evolution requires workers to adapt, acquire digital literacy, and develop skills that complement automation technologies.

The future of work in the service industry will be marked by collaboration between humans and automation, with employees focusing on tasks that require creativity, problem-solving, and emotional intelligence, while machines handle routine and data-driven functions.

In the following sections, we'll delve deeper into the changing landscape of specific job roles within the service industry and explore strategies for those seeking to thrive in this automated environment. Understanding the role of automation in reshaping these sectors is essential for both businesses and individuals seeking to navigate the shifting landscape of service-related jobs.

THE WHITE-COLLAR IMPACT

Automation has made significant inroads into white-collar jobs, transforming the landscape of professional and administrative roles. These roles, once synonymous with job security and stability, are now being redefined by the Automation Wave.

1. Administrative and Office Automation

1.1. **Administrative and Office Automation:** The backbone of many organizations, administrative roles have seen significant changes due to automation.

1.2. **Robotic Process Automation (RPA):** RPA software automates repetitive, rule-based tasks in office environments, such as data entry, invoicing, and document management.

1.3. **Email Sorting and Filtering:** Automation algorithms categorize and prioritize emails, helping professionals manage their inboxes efficiently.

1.4. **Virtual Assistants:** Virtual assistants, powered by AI and natural language processing, can schedule appointments, draft emails, and provide reminders.

1.5. **Data Analytics:** Automation tools analyse vast datasets, extracting insights and generating reports with minimal human intervention.

2. **Financial and Accounting Automation**

2.1. **Financial and Accounting Automation:** In the realm of finance and accounting, automation technologies have reshaped how financial tasks are performed.

2.2. **Algorithmic Trading:** Automated algorithms execute financial trades based on predefined criteria, optimizing trading processes.

2.3. **Bookkeeping Software:** Accounting software automates ledger entries and reconciliations, reducing the manual workload for accountants.

2.4. **Expense Management:** Automated expense management tools simplify the process of submitting, reviewing, and reimbursing expenses.

2.5. **Audit Automation:** Audit software uses data analytics and automation to enhance the efficiency and accuracy of auditing processes.

3. Legal Industry Automation

3.1. **Legal Industry Automation:** Automation has found a place in the legal field, transforming legal research and document management.

3.2. **Legal Research Tools:** Automation helps legal professionals search, review, and analyse vast volumes of case law and statutes.

3.3. **Document Review and Management:** Machine learning algorithms assist in the review and management of legal documents, streamlining the work of paralegals and attorneys.

3.4. **Contract Analysis:** AI-powered tools can extract and analyse key information from contracts, helping legal professionals review agreements efficiently.

4. Healthcare and Medical Records Automation

4.1. **Healthcare and Medical Records Automation:** In healthcare, automation is enhancing administrative tasks and improving patient care.

4.2. **Electronic Health Records (EHRs):** EHR systems automate the collection, storage, and management of patient health data, streamlining healthcare administration.

4.3. **Medical Coding Automation:** Automated coding software assists medical professionals in assigning appropriate codes to diagnoses and procedures for billing and insurance purposes.

4.4. **Medication Dispensing Robots:** In healthcare facilities, robots are used to dispense medications and manage inventory.

The Impact on White-Collar Jobs

The impact of automation on white-collar jobs is multifaceted. On one hand, it offers the potential to improve productivity, reduce errors, and free up professionals from repetitive tasks, allowing them to focus on more strategic and value-added responsibilities.

On the other hand, it raises concerns about job displacement, especially in roles that involve routine and data-intensive tasks. For workers in white-collar professions, the challenge lies in adapting to a landscape where automation complements their skills rather than replaces them.

As white-collar roles evolve, there's an increasing demand for skills that complement automation technologies. Skills such as critical thinking, problem-solving, data interpretation, and complex decision-making are becoming more valuable. Professionals are encouraged to embrace lifelong learning and upskilling to stay competitive in an automated job market.

In the sections that follow, we'll delve deeper into the specific impacts of automation on various white-collar job roles and explore strategies for those seeking to thrive in this evolving landscape. Understanding the role of automation in reshaping white-collar professions is crucial for both workers and organizations in navigating the shifting terrain of professional jobs.

IMPLICATIONS FOR TRANSPORTATION AND LOGISTICS

The transportation and logistics industry plays a pivotal role in the global economy, facilitating the movement of goods and people. Automation technologies are significantly impacting this sector, ushering in both opportunities and challenges.

1. Autonomous Vehicles

1.1. **Autonomous Vehicles:** Automation has a profound impact on the future of transportation, with autonomous vehicles at the forefront.

1.2. **Self-Driving Cars:** Autonomous cars have the potential to transform personal transportation. They promise improved safety, reduced traffic congestion, and increased accessibility for those unable to drive.

1.3. **Autonomous Trucks:** The trucking industry is exploring self-driving trucks for long-haul freight transportation, which could lead to increased efficiency and reduced transportation costs.

2. Last-Mile Delivery

2.1. **Last-Mile Delivery:** The final leg of delivery to the customer's doorstep is an area where automation is making significant strides.

2.2. **Delivery Drones:** Companies are experimenting with delivery drones to carry small packages directly to customers' homes, especially in areas with challenging terrain or traffic.

2.3. **Robotic Delivery Vehicles:** Autonomous robots and small vehicles are being used for last-mile delivery in urban environments. They can navigate sidewalks and traffic to deliver goods quickly.

3. Warehouse Automation

3.1. **Warehouse Automation:** Logistics and distribution centres are embracing automation technologies to improve efficiency and reduce labour costs.

3.2. **Automated Sorting Systems:** Conveyor belts, robots, and automated sorting systems expedite the process of categorizing and packaging goods for distribution.

3.3. **Autonomous Forklifts:** Self-driving forklifts and material handling equipment streamline warehouse operations, from picking and packing to inventory management.

3.4. **Inventory Management Systems:** Automation tools optimize inventory control, ensuring that stock levels are accurate and reducing the risk of overstock or stockouts.

4. Supply Chain Visibility and Optimization

4.1. **Supply Chain Visibility and Optimization:** Automation enhances the transparency and efficiency of supply chain management.

4.2. **IoT Sensors:** Internet of Things (IoT) sensors monitor the location and condition of goods in transit, providing real-time data for supply chain optimization.

4.3. **Predictive Analytics:** Automation tools use predictive analytics to anticipate demand fluctuations, enabling more efficient allocation of resources and inventory.

4.4. **Blockchain:** Distributed ledger technology like blockchain offers a transparent and secure platform for tracking the provenance and status of goods in the supply chain.

5. The Impact on Jobs and Workers

Automation in transportation and logistics is redefining job roles and requiring the workforce to adapt to new technologies. While automation presents opportunities for increased efficiency and reduced costs, it also raises concerns about job displacement.

5.1. **Truck Drivers:** Autonomous trucks have the potential to reduce the demand for long-haul truck drivers. However, there may still be a need for drivers for local delivery and other tasks.

5.2. **Delivery Personnel:** Last-mile delivery automation may change the nature of delivery jobs, with workers overseeing and maintaining delivery drones or robotic vehicles.

5.3. **Warehouse Workers:** Automation in warehouses may lead to a shift in job roles, with workers overseeing and maintaining automated systems and focusing on more complex tasks.

5.4. **Supply Chain Professionals:** Professionals in supply chain management may need to adapt to new technologies, such as IoT sensors and blockchain, to optimize supply chain operations.

5.5. **Data Analysts:** The growing use of automation generates vast amounts of data that require analysis and interpretation, leading to increased demand for data analysts.

Navigating this transformation requires reskilling and upskilling for workers in the transportation and logistics industry. It also calls for a proactive approach to integrating automation technologies into supply chain and transportation operations, ensuring that organizations can reap the benefits of increased efficiency and sustainability.

In the following sections, we'll delve deeper into the specific impacts of automation on various job roles within the transportation and logistics sector and explore strategies for those seeking to thrive in this evolving landscape. Understanding the role of automation in reshaping transportation and logistics is essential for both workers and organizations in adapting to the shifting terrain of this crucial industry.

THE CREATIVE DILEMMA

Creativity has long been celebrated as a unique human trait, one that is closely associated with art, design, writing, and various forms of expression. However, automation technologies are challenging the boundaries of creativity and ushering in a creative dilemma.

1. Automation in Creative Industries

1.1. **Automation in Creative Industries:** The creative industries, which include advertising, design, content creation, and more, are not immune to the impact of automation.

1.2. **Graphic Design:** Automation tools can generate graphics, layouts, and even logos, reducing the need for manual design work.

1.3. **Copywriting:** AI-powered writing tools can create marketing copy, news articles, and social media posts, often indistinguishable from content written by humans.

1.4. **Video and Audio Editing:** Automation is simplifying the video and audio editing process, enabling creators to generate content more efficiently.

2. The Impact on Creativity

2.1. **The Impact on Creativity:** Automation technologies can perform creative tasks, but they also raise questions about the authenticity of creative work.

2.2. **Consistency vs. Uniqueness:** Automation tools can produce consistent, high-quality content, but the risk is that content may become formulaic and lack the unique touch of human creativity.

2.3. **The Human Element:** Human creators bring personal experiences, emotions, and nuanced perspectives to their work, making it distinct and relatable. Automation lacks this human touch.

2.4. **Collaboration:** Some creators are learning to collaborate with automation tools, using them to augment their creative processes. This fusion of human and machine creativity is a growing trend.

3. Reskilling and New Opportunities

3.1. **Reskilling and New Opportunities:** The creative dilemma pushes creative professionals to adapt and explore new horizons.

3.2. **Creative Data Analysis:** As automation generates data, there is a growing need for professionals who can analyse and interpret this data creatively.

3.3. **AI-Assisted Creativity:** Some creative professionals are learning to harness automation tools to enhance their work, using AI to generate initial ideas or designs.

4. **Embracing Hybrid Roles:** Hybrid roles that blend creativity with technology are emerging. For example, "creative technologists" are skilled in both creative arts and technology.

5. Ethical Considerations

5.1. **Ethical Considerations:** The use of automation in creative work also raises ethical questions.

5.2. **Plagiarism and Attribution:** When automated content is used, issues of plagiarism and proper attribution must be addressed.

5.3. **Data Privacy:** The use of data in creative content raises concerns about data privacy and the ethical handling of personal information.

5.4. **Authenticity and Transparency:** Creators and organizations must be transparent about the use of automation in their content to maintain authenticity and trust.

The creative dilemma is a nuanced challenge. Automation technologies have the potential to enhance efficiency and broaden the scope of creative work. Still, they also pose questions about the essence of creativity and the need for a human touch in artistic and expressive endeavours.

In the following sections, we'll delve deeper into the specific impacts of automation on creative roles and explore strategies for creative professionals seeking to thrive in this changing landscape. Understanding the role of automation in reshaping creativity is crucial for both creators and organizations seeking to navigate the complexities of the creative industry in the age of automation.

THE HUMAN TOUCH: JOBS AUTOMATION CAN'T REPLACE

While automation technologies have made significant inroads into various industries and job roles, there are certain aspects of work that remain uniquely human. These "human touch" jobs rely on emotional intelligence, creativity, complex problem-solving, and interpersonal skills that automation struggles to replicate.

1. Healthcare and Patient Care

1.1. **Healthcare and Patient Care:** The healthcare industry is a prime example of an area where human touch is irreplaceable.

1.2. **Compassionate Patient Care:** Healthcare professionals, such as nurses and doctors, provide compassionate care and emotional support to patients during times of illness and distress.

1.3. **Complex Diagnoses:** Diagnosing complex medical conditions often requires a deep understanding of a patient's history, emotions, and overall well-being, which goes beyond data analysis.

1.4. **Mental Health and Therapy:** Mental health professionals, including therapists and counsellors, provide a safe and empathetic space for individuals to address their emotional and psychological well-being.

2. Education and Mentorship

2.1. **Education and Mentorship:** The education sector relies heavily on the human touch for effective learning and development.

2.2. **Personalized Teaching:** Educators can adapt their teaching methods to suit the unique needs and learning styles of individual students, offering one-on-one guidance and mentorship.

2.3. **Emotional Support:** Teachers play a pivotal role in providing emotional support, encouragement, and a nurturing environment for students, particularly in their formative years.

2.4. **Mentoring and Career Guidance:** Career mentors and counsellors offer personalized guidance and advice that considers an individual's aspirations, values, and life circumstances.

3. Creative Arts and Expression

3.1. **Creative Arts and Expression:** In creative industries, the human touch is essential for authentic and meaningful work.

3.2. **Artistic Expression:** Artists, writers, musicians, and performers bring their personal experiences and emotions into their work, creating unique and evocative pieces that resonate with audiences.

3.3. **Creative Problem-Solving:** Creative professionals often engage in complex problem-solving and conceptual thinking that transcends algorithmic or formulaic solutions.

3.4. **Cultural Preservation:** The preservation of cultural heritage and traditions often relies on the expertise and passion of individuals who are deeply connected to their culture.

4. Human Resources and People Management

4.1. **Human Resources and People Management:** Roles in human resources and people management require interpersonal skills and understanding.

4.2. **Conflict Resolution:** HR professionals are skilled in mediating conflicts and addressing workplace disputes, which involves a nuanced understanding of human emotions.

4.3. **Employee Development:** Employee development and engagement require tailored approaches that consider individual needs and career goals.

4.4. **Leadership and Team Building:** Effective leaders and team managers create environments that foster collaboration, trust, and a sense of belonging.

5. **Social Services and Community Support**

5.1. **Social Services and Community Support:** The human touch is central to the field of social services and community support.

5.2. **Social Work:** Social workers provide emotional support, advocacy, and practical assistance to individuals and families facing challenges, such as poverty, abuse, or addiction.

5.3. **Community Building:** Community organizers and activists work to build strong, connected communities, relying on their understanding of local culture and the needs of the people they serve.

5.4. **Empowerment and Advocacy:** Advocacy roles require empathetic and skilled individuals who can represent the interests and rights of marginalized or vulnerable populations.

These "human touch" jobs highlight the areas where human qualities such as empathy, intuition, creativity, and moral judgment are not easily replaced by automation. While technology can support these roles, it is often in a complementary capacity, allowing professionals to focus on the uniquely human aspects of their work. Recognizing the value of the human touch is not just essential for job security; it is crucial for maintaining the quality of care, education, creativity, and support in our societies. In the sections that follow, we'll explore strategies for individuals in "human touch" jobs to leverage automation as a supportive tool while preserving the core values that make these roles indispensable to society.

THE TRANSFORMATION OF EDUCATION

Education is at the heart of societal progress, and it too is undergoing a significant transformation due to the influence of automation and digital technologies. This transformation is reshaping how we teach, learn, and prepare students for a world where automation and AI play an increasingly prominent role.

1. Online Learning and Digital Classrooms

1.1. **Online Learning and Digital Classrooms:** One of the most noticeable shifts in education is the rise of online learning and digital classrooms.

1.2. **E-Learning Platforms:** Online platforms and learning management systems offer a wide range of courses and educational content, accessible from anywhere in the world.

1.3. **Virtual Classrooms:** Video conferencing tools enable students and educators to engage in real-time classes, fostering remote education and collaboration.

1.4. **Adaptive Learning:** Algorithms analyse students' progress and adapt course content to their needs, enhancing personalized learning experiences.

2. Artificial Intelligence in Education

2.1. **Artificial Intelligence in Education:** AI is being integrated into educational technology, offering various benefits.

2.2. **Personalized Learning Paths:** AI can analyse students' learning styles and needs, adjusting the curriculum and learning materials to optimize their progress.

2.3. **Smart Content Creation:** AI-driven tools can generate educational content, from lesson plans to quiz questions, saving educators time and enhancing content quality.

2.4. **Early Intervention:** AI systems can identify struggling students and provide early intervention, offering additional support to help them catch up.

3. Skill Development for the Future

3.1. **Skill Development for the Future:** The changing landscape of work demands that education focuses on future-ready skills.

3.2. **Critical Thinking and Problem-Solving:** These skills are vital for navigating the complexities of the modern world and adapting to rapidly evolving industries.

3.3. **Digital Literacy:** Proficiency in using digital tools, understanding cybersecurity, and navigating online resources is increasingly important.

3.4. **Collaboration and Communication:** Effective teamwork and communication are crucial in a globalized, interconnected workforce.

4. Hybrid Learning Environments

4.1. **Hybrid Learning Environments:** Many educational institutions are adopting hybrid models that combine in-person and online learning.

4.2. **Flipped Classrooms:** In a flipped classroom, students engage with course materials online before in-person classes, allowing class time to focus on discussion and application.

4.3. **Blended Learning:** Blended learning combines online and in-person components to create a flexible and adaptable educational experience.

4.4. **Virtual Labs and Simulations:** Virtual labs and simulations provide hands-on experiences for subjects that traditionally required physical resources.

5. **Preparing Students for the Automation Age**

   5.1. **Preparing Students for the Automation Age:** Education is evolving to equip students with the skills and mindset needed for an automated future.

   5.2. **Problem-Solving Over Memorization:** The emphasis is shifting from memorization to problem-solving, encouraging students to think critically and apply knowledge.

   5.3. **Coding and Digital Literacy: Basic** coding skills and digital literacy are becoming fundamental, even for students who do not intend to pursue tech careers.

   5.4. **Soft Skills and Emotional Intelligence:** The importance of soft skills, including emotional intelligence, is growing as they are more challenging for automation to replicate.

6. **Lifelong Learning and Reskilling**

   6.1. **Lifelong Learning and Reskilling:** Education is extending beyond formal institutions, with an emphasis on continuous learning and upskilling.

6.2. **Online Courses and Micro credentials:** Online platforms offer courses and micro credentials that allow individuals to acquire new skills and credentials at their own pace.

6.3. **Reskilling Programs:** Organizations are investing in reskilling programs to help employees adapt to changing job roles and industry demands.

6.4. **Mentorship and Coaching:** Mentorship and coaching programs connect experienced professionals with learners seeking guidance and support.

The transformation of education is a response to the rapidly changing job landscape and the need to prepare students for roles that may not yet exist. By embracing technology and focusing on developing skills that complement automation, education is evolving to create a more adaptable and future-ready workforce. In the following sections, we'll explore the specific ways in which education is changing and provide insights for students, educators, and institutions looking to navigate this evolving landscape successfully.

EMBRACING CHANGE

In the midst of the seismic shifts brought about by automation and technology, one thing is certain: change is the new constant. To navigate this transformative landscape successfully, individuals, organizations, and industries must not only adapt but embrace change as a driving force for growth and innovation.

1. Adaptability as a Core Skill

1.1. **Adaptability as a Core Skill:** In an era of rapid change, adaptability is not just a nice-to-have skill; it's essential.

1.2. **Learning Agility:** Learning how to learn, and doing so quickly, is a cornerstone of adaptability. It involves being open to new information and skills.

1.3. **Resilience:** Resilience is the capacity to withstand adversity and bounce back from setbacks. It's a crucial quality for navigating change.

1.4. **Mindset Shift:** Adopting a growth mindset, which embraces challenges and sees failure as an opportunity for growth, is fundamental.

2. Continuous Learning and Upskilling

2.1. **Continuous Learning and Upskilling:** Lifelong learning is the new norm, and upskilling is a necessity.

2.2. **Online Courses:** The availability of online courses and resources makes learning accessible and convenient, whether it's acquiring a new skill or updating existing ones.

2.3. **Micro credentials:** Micro credentials and digital badges offer targeted, industry-specific learning and recognition.

2.4. **Reskilling Programs:** Employers are investing in reskilling programs to help employees adapt to changing job roles and technology.

3. Collaboration and Interdisciplinary Work

3.1. **Collaboration and Interdisciplinary Work:** Collaboration across disciplines and industries can spark innovation and provide fresh perspectives.

3.2. **Interdisciplinary Teams:** Teams with members from diverse backgrounds, experiences, and skills are more likely to generate innovative solutions.

3.3. **Cross-Industry Insights:** Insights from other industries can be a valuable source of inspiration for solving challenges in one's own field.

3.4. **Open Innovation:** Embracing open innovation and collaborative partnerships can lead to breakthroughs that are otherwise unattainable.

4. Fostering Creativity and Innovation

4.1. **Fostering Creativity and Innovation:** Creativity and innovation drive progress and adaptation.

4.2. **Creative Problem-Solving:** Encouraging creative problem-solving and design thinking can lead to more effective solutions.

4.3. **Innovation Labs:** Many organizations establish innovation labs or hubs to foster a culture of experimentation and innovation.

4.4. **Prototyping and Testing:** Rapid prototyping and testing of ideas allow for quick feedback and improvement.

5. Ethical Considerations and Responsible AI

5.1. Ethical Considerations and Responsible AI: As automation technologies become more prevalent, ethical considerations become paramount.

5.2. Ethical AI: Ensuring that AI and automation systems are designed and used ethically is essential to avoid unintended consequences.

5.3. Data Privacy: Protecting data privacy and securing sensitive information is an ethical imperative in an increasingly data-driven world.

5.4. Transparency and Accountability: Transparency and accountability in the use of automation technologies are essential for building trust.

6. Preparing for the Unknown

6.1. Preparing for the Unknown: The future is unpredictable, so preparing for the unknown is a necessity.

6.2. Scenario Planning: Scenario planning helps organizations anticipate and prepare for various possible futures.

6.3. **Agile Strategies:** Adopting agile strategies allows organizations to pivot quickly in response to changing circumstances.

6.4. **Innovation Culture:** Nurturing a culture of innovation and experimentation prepares organizations to adapt to unexpected changes.

Embracing change is not just a matter of survival; it's an opportunity for growth and advancement. By fostering adaptability, continuous learning, and a culture of innovation, individuals and organizations can thrive in the age of automation. Furthermore, approaching change with a sense of responsibility, ethics, and a collaborative mindset ensures that we harness the power of automation for the benefit of society as a whole.

In the following sections, we'll explore specific strategies and examples of how individuals and organizations are successfully embracing change and thriving in this era of automation and transformation.

CONCLUSION: EMBRACING THE AUTOMATION AGE

In this exploration of the Automation Age, we have journeyed through the profound impact of automation on traditional jobs, industries, and the very nature of work itself. We have uncovered the far-reaching consequences of this technological revolution and discovered that, rather than resist change, we must embrace it and adapt to the evolving landscape.

The Impact of Automation on Traditional Jobs:

The pages of this book have unveiled the profound transformations that automation has brought to traditional jobs. As repetitive tasks yield to the efficiency of machines, the human workforce finds itself at a crossroads. Automation, while displacing some roles, also opens doors to new possibilities. The jobs that automation can't replace are those that require a uniquely human touch—empathy, creativity, and complex problem-solving. As we've witnessed, these irreplaceable qualities are essential in healthcare, education, creative arts, and various other domains.

Looking Ahead to the Future of Work:

The future of work is not a distant horizon; it's unfolding before our eyes. It's a future marked by agility, adaptability, and a commitment to lifelong learning. The Automation Age has revolutionized industries, creating a demand for digital skills and tech-savvy professionals. This transformation presents boundless opportunities for innovation, from autonomous vehicles to AI-powered healthcare. As the boundaries of work blur, the gig economy, remote work, and the hybrid workforce are redefining our concepts of employment. Moreover, the ethical use of automation is increasingly relevant in a world where technology intersects with every facet of our lives.

The Need for Continuous Learning and Adaptability in a Changing Job Market:

The fundamental lesson of the Automation Age is that learning never stops. Adaptability and the capacity to acquire new skills are not just advantages—they are prerequisites for thriving in this ever-shifting landscape. Continuous learning and upskilling are the tools that ensure we remain relevant, no matter how our industries change. Lifelong learning is not only a personal endeavour but a collective one, as organizations and educational institutions adapt to meet the demands of the future workforce.

As we conclude our journey through the Automation Age, let's embrace this pivotal moment in history with open arms and open minds. The Automation Wave is not a force to resist, but a tide to ride. The future of work is ours to shape, and the skills we develop today will chart the course for tomorrow.

Acknowledging the impact of automation on traditional jobs, looking ahead to the future of work, and embracing the need for continuous learning and adaptability are the keys to not just surviving but thriving in the Automation Age. So, let's meet the future head-on, with curiosity, resilience, and an unyielding commitment to progress.

EMBRACING CHANGE: THE MINDSET OF A FUTURE-READY PROFESSIONAL

In our journey through the ever-evolving landscape of tech careers and the Automation Age, one thing has become abundantly clear: change is the new constant, and adaptability is the true currency of success. To thrive in the age of automation and technological advancement, cultivating a mindset of readiness for the future is not just a choice; it's a necessity.

1. The Growth Mindset

1.1. **The Growth Mindset:** At the heart of a future-ready professional's mindset is the growth mindset. This perspective sees challenges and failures as opportunities for learning and growth.

1.2. **Embracing Challenges:** Instead of shying away from challenges, future-ready professionals seek them out as chances to expand their skills and knowledge.

1.3. **Resilience:** Resilience in the face of setbacks is a hallmark of the growth mindset. It's the understanding that failure is not the end, but a stepping stone to success.

1.4. **Continuous Learning:** The commitment to continuous learning is an inherent part of the growth mindset. It's the belief that there is always more to discover and absorb.

2. Agility and Adaptability

2.1. **Agility and Adaptability:** In the Automation Age, the ability to pivot and adapt quickly is invaluable.

2.2. **Learning Agility:** Future-ready professionals not only learn but learn how to learn. They adapt rapidly to new information and technologies.

2.3. **Interdisciplinary Thinking:** The willingness to cross boundaries and explore diverse fields and perspectives is a vital part of adaptability.

2.4. **Tech Savviness:** In a world where technology is omnipresent, tech savviness is a must. It involves not only using technology but understanding it and leveraging it effectively.

3. Innovation and Creativity

3.1. **Innovation and Creativity:** Future-ready professionals foster a culture of innovation and creativity, recognizing that these qualities drive progress.

3.2. **Creative Problem-Solving:** The ability to think outside the box and generate innovative solutions is a hallmark of future-ready professionals.

3.3. **Open-Mindedness:** Being open to new ideas and alternative approaches fosters creativity and innovation.

3.4. **Experimentation and Risk-Taking:** Future-ready professionals are willing to experiment and take calculated risks to drive innovation and change.

4. Collaboration and Inclusivity

4.1. **Collaboration and Inclusivity:** In a highly interconnected world, collaboration and a spirit of inclusivity are essential.

4.2. **Cross-Disciplinary Collaboration:** Future-ready professionals value cross-disciplinary collaboration, recognizing that diverse perspectives lead to innovation.

4.3. **Cultural Competence:** Understanding and respecting different cultures and perspectives is crucial in a globalized world.

4.4. **Inclusive Leadership:** Leadership that values inclusivity and fosters a sense of belonging is a hallmark of future-ready professionals.

5. Responsible Use of Technology

5.1. **Responsible Use of Technology:** In an era where technology has immense power, a commitment to ethical and responsible use of technology is paramount.

5.2. **Ethical AI and Automation:** Future-ready professionals ensure that technology is used in a way that aligns with ethical principles and respects human rights.

5.3. **Data Privacy:** Protecting data privacy and safeguarding sensitive information is a top priority in a tech-driven world.

5.4. **Transparency and Accountability:** Operating with transparency and being accountable for the use of technology is essential for building trust.

In the age of automation, the mindset of a future-ready professional is not just about being a spectator; it's about being an active participant in shaping the future. Embracing change, fostering adaptability, and nurturing a growth mindset are the pillars of success in this era.

As we navigate the shifting landscape of tech careers and the ever-evolving world of automation, let's remember that the future belongs to those who are willing to embrace change with open arms. The Automation Age is not a threat, but an opportunity for progress, innovation, and personal and professional growth.

So, as you conclude this journey through the future of tech careers, embrace the mindset of a future-ready professional, and let it guide you as you navigate the ever-changing terrain of the Automation Age. In this age, the future belongs to those who stand ready to seize it.

THE RISE OF AI AND ITS ROLE IN THE JOB MARKET

Artificial Intelligence (AI) has emerged as one of the most transformative technologies of our time, and its impact on the job market is profound. From automating routine tasks to creating entirely new job roles, AI is reshaping the world of work in ways that demand our attention and adaptation.

1. Automation and Task-Based Jobs

1.1. **Automation and Task-Based Jobs:** AI's role in automation is perhaps the most visible and disruptive aspect of its impact on the job market.

1.2. **Routine Tasks:** Jobs that involve repetitive and predictable tasks, such as data entry, manufacturing, and simple data analysis, are being automated at a rapid pace.

1.3. **Efficiency and Productivity:** AI-powered automation systems enhance efficiency and productivity, but they also raise concerns about job displacement.

1.4. **Shift in Skill Requirements:** As routine tasks are automated, there is a growing demand for higher-order skills such as problem-solving, creativity, and emotional intelligence.

2. AI Augmentation and Human-AI Collaboration

2.1. **AI Augmentation and Human-AI Collaboration:** AI isn't just a job disruptor; it's also a powerful tool for enhancing human capabilities.

2.2. **Augmenting Decision-Making:** AI aids in complex decision-making processes by analyzing vast datasets and generating insights that humans might overlook.

2.3. **Predictive Analytics:** AI systems use predictive analytics to forecast trends, customer behavior, and market dynamics, enabling better business strategies.

2.4. **AI-Enhanced Creativity:** Creative professionals use AI tools to generate content ideas, design concepts, and even music, expanding their creative horizons.

3. New Job Roles and Industries

3.1. **New Job Roles and Industries:** AI is not only changing existing jobs; it's also creating entirely new job roles and industries.

3.2. **AI Ethics and Compliance:** The rise of AI has led to the emergence of roles focused on AI ethics, compliance, and responsible AI development.

3.3. **Data Science and AI Specialists:** Data scientists, AI engineers, and machine learning specialists are in high demand as organizations seek to harness the power of AI.

3.4. **AI-Generated Content Creators:** AI-powered content creators, chatbots, and virtual assistants are creating job roles for AI content managers and trainers.

4. Soft Skills and Emotional Intelligence

4.1. **Soft Skills and Emotional Intelligence:** As AI takes on routine tasks, soft skills and emotional intelligence are becoming more critical in the job market.

4.2. **Communication and Collaboration:** Effective communication and collaboration skills are in demand as teams become more diverse and dispersed.

4.3. **Empathy and Emotional Intelligence:** Jobs that require empathy, understanding, and emotional intelligence, such as counseling, healthcare, and customer support, are on the rise.

4.4. **Problem-Solving and Critical Thinking:** Analytical and critical thinking skills are essential in addressing complex, non-routine challenges.

5. Education and Upskilling

5.1. **Education and Upskilling:** As AI transforms the job market, education and upskilling are essential for individuals and organizations to stay competitive.

5.2. **Continuous Learning:** Lifelong learning is no longer optional; it's a requirement for keeping skills up to date in a rapidly evolving job market.

5.3. **Reskilling Programs:** Organizations are investing in reskilling programs to help employees adapt to the changing job landscape.

5.4. **Tech Literacy:** Basic technology literacy is increasingly vital, even for jobs that were once considered non-technical.

The rise of AI is not just a technological revolution; it's a transformation of the very fabric of work. AI-driven automation is redefining job roles, creating new industries, and placing a premium on uniquely human skills. The ability to adapt, upskill, and collaborate with AI is the key to success in this evolving job market.

As we conclude this exploration of AI's role in the job market, let's remember that while AI is a powerful tool, it's humans who wield it. The future of work is not about humans versus AI but about humans working alongside AI, leveraging its capabilities while contributing the uniquely human qualities that make us indispensable in the workforce.

CLOUD COMPUTING AND THE NEW HORIZONS OF DATA MANAGEMENT

Cloud computing has revolutionized the way organizations manage and leverage their data. It offers unparalleled scalability, flexibility, and accessibility, changing the landscape of data storage, analysis, and utilization. In this section, we'll explore how cloud computing is shaping the future of data management and its impact on various aspects of our professional lives.

1. Scalability and Accessibility

1.1. **Scalability and Accessibility:** Cloud computing provides virtually limitless scalability and unprecedented accessibility to data.

1.2. **Scalable Infrastructure:** Organizations can effortlessly scale their computing and storage resources up or down to meet fluctuating demands.

1.3. **Global Accessibility:** Cloud services can be accessed from anywhere with an internet connection, enabling remote work and global collaboration.

1.4. **Reduced Infrastructure Costs:** Cloud services reduce the need for on-premises data centres and associated infrastructure costs.

2. Big Data and Analytics

2.1. **Big Data and Analytics:** Cloud computing empowers organizations to harness big data and extract valuable insights.

2.2. **Data Storage and Processing:** The cloud offers the capacity to store and process vast amounts of data, enabling advanced analytics and machine learning.

2.3. **Real-Time Analysis:** Cloud-based analytics platforms can provide real-time insights into business operations, customer behavior, and market trends.

3. **Data Visualization:** Cloud-based tools make data visualization and reporting more accessible, aiding in decision-making.

4. Data Security and Compliance

4.1. **Data Security and Compliance:** Cloud providers prioritize data security and compliance, offering robust solutions.

4.2. **Data Encryption:** Data is encrypted both in transit and at rest, ensuring its security.

4.3. **Compliance Standards:** Cloud providers adhere to industry-specific compliance standards, which simplifies compliance for organizations.

4.4. **Access Controls:** Granular access controls enable organizations to manage who can access and modify data.

5. Data Collaboration and Sharing

5.1. **Data Collaboration and Sharing:** Cloud computing facilitates collaboration and data sharing.

5.2. **Real-Time Collaboration:** Cloud-based tools enable real-time collaboration, allowing teams to work on data simultaneously.

5.3. **Secure Sharing:** Cloud platforms offer secure sharing mechanisms, ensuring data is shared only with authorized users.

5.4. **Version Control:** Version control features track changes and revisions, aiding in data management.

6. Disaster Recovery and Business Continuity

6.1. Disaster Recovery and Business Continuity: The cloud provides robust disaster recovery and business continuity solutions.

6.2. Data Redundancy: Data is replicated across multiple data centres, minimizing the risk of data loss due to hardware failures or disasters.

6.3. Quick Recovery: Cloud-based disaster recovery solutions enable swift data recovery in case of unexpected incidents.

6.4. Cost Efficiency: Cloud-based disaster recovery is often more cost-effective than traditional methods.

7. The Future of Data-Driven Work

7.1. The Future of Data-Driven Work: Cloud computing is at the forefront of the data-driven future of work.

7.2. IoT and Edge Computing: The cloud supports the data influx from IoT devices and edge computing, powering new applications and services.

7.3. **AI and Machine Learning:** Cloud-based AI and machine learning services are becoming instrumental in data analysis and automation.

7.4. **Hybrid and Multi-Cloud Environments:** Organizations are increasingly adopting hybrid and multi-cloud strategies to optimize their data management and workloads.

The rise of cloud computing is a transformative force in data management. It enables organizations to not only efficiently store and analyse data but also collaborate, ensure security and compliance, and implement disaster recovery solutions. As cloud computing continues to evolve, it will play an increasingly pivotal role in the way we manage and leverage data, shaping the horizons of data-driven work and innovation.

CRYPTOCURRENCY AND BLOCKCHAIN: REVOLUTIONIZING FINANCE AND BEYOND

Cryptocurrency and blockchain technology have emerged as transformative forces, disrupted traditional financial systems and offered possibilities that extend far beyond the world of finance. In this section, we'll delve into how cryptocurrency and blockchain are reshaping our understanding of money, transactions, and the very foundations of trust.

1. The Rise of Cryptocurrency

1.1. **The Rise of Cryptocurrency:** Cryptocurrency represents a paradigm shift in the way we think about money and transactions.

1.2. **Digital Currency:** Cryptocurrency is purely digital, enabling secure and borderless transactions.

1.3. **Decentralization:** Cryptocurrencies are often decentralized, meaning they operate on a peer-to-peer network without a central authority.

1.4. **Security and Transparency:** Blockchain technology underpins cryptocurrencies, ensuring security and transparency in transactions.

2. Blockchain: The Technology Behind Cryptocurrency

2.1. **Blockchain:** The Technology Behind Cryptocurrency: Blockchain is the ledger technology that makes cryptocurrency transactions possible.

2.2. **Immutable Ledger:** Blockchain records are permanent and tamper-resistant, enhancing trust in transactions.

2.3. **Smart Contracts:** Blockchain can execute smart contracts, self-executing agreements that automate actions upon meeting predefined conditions.

2.4. **Supply Chain Management:** Blockchain's transparency and traceability are used in supply chain management to enhance accountability.

3. Financial Inclusion and Accessibility

3.1. **Financial Inclusion and Accessibility:** Cryptocurrency has the potential to bring financial services to the unbanked and underbanked populations.

3.2. **Global Access:** Cryptocurrencies can be accessed by anyone with an internet connection, transcending geographic and institutional boundaries.

3.3. **Low Transaction Costs:** Cryptocurrency transactions often have lower fees, reducing the financial burden on users.

3.4. **Cross-Border Transactions:** Cryptocurrency simplifies cross-border payments, making international trade and remittances more efficient.

4. Disrupting Traditional Finance

4.1. **Disrupting Traditional Finance:** Cryptocurrency challenges traditional financial systems and institutions.

4.2. **Decentralized Finance (DeFi):** DeFi platforms use blockchain to offer financial services like lending, borrowing, and trading without traditional intermediaries.

4.3. **Central Bank Digital Currencies (CBDCs):** Some central banks are exploring the development of their own digital currencies, further blurring the lines between traditional and digital finance.

4.4. **Tokenization:** Real-world assets, such as real estate and art, are being tokenized and traded on blockchain platforms, increasing accessibility and liquidity.

5. Beyond Finance: Blockchain's Wider Applications

5.1. **Beyond Finance:** Blockchain's Wider Applications: Blockchain's utility goes beyond finance, extending into various sectors.

5.2. **Healthcare:** Blockchain ensures secure and interoperable health records, streamlining patient care and research.

5.3. **Supply Chain:** Blockchain verifies the authenticity and origin of products, combating counterfeiting and ensuring quality.

5.4. **Voting and Governance:** Blockchain can enable secure and transparent voting and governance systems, enhancing democracy.

6. The Future of Finance and Beyond

6.1. **The Future of Finance and Beyond:** Cryptocurrency and blockchain are on the cusp of transformative changes in various sectors.

6.2. **Regulation and Compliance:** The regulatory landscape is evolving to accommodate cryptocurrency, ensuring security and consumer protection.

6.3. **Sustainability:** The environmental impact of cryptocurrency mining is a growing concern, driving efforts to make it more sustainable.

6.4. **Interoperability:** The challenge of interoperability between various blockchain networks and cryptocurrencies is being addressed to create a more interconnected ecosystem.

Cryptocurrency and blockchain technology are ushering in a new era of finance and trust, as well as reaching far beyond the financial sector. Their potential to foster financial inclusion, disrupt traditional systems, and underpin transparent transactions has ramifications across industries and sectors. Understanding and harnessing the power of cryptocurrency and blockchain is essential for businesses and individuals looking to navigate the future with a grasp of these transformative technologies.

WEB3 AND THE FUTURE OF THE INTERNET

The internet has evolved dramatically since its inception, and Web3 represents the next phase in this ongoing transformation. Web3, often referred to as the decentralized web, is reimagining the internet, shifting power from central authorities to users and communities. In this section, we'll explore how Web3 is revolutionizing the internet, its core principles, and its potential impact on various aspects of our digital lives.

1. Decentralization and User Empowerment

1.1. **Decentralization and User Empowerment:** Web3 is built on principles of decentralization, putting users in control of their online experiences.

1.2. **Peer-to-Peer Networks:** Web3 relies on decentralized, peer-to-peer networks that eliminate central intermediaries.

1.3. **Ownership of Data:** Users have greater ownership and control over their data, deciding who accesses it and how it's used.

1.4. **Blockchain Technology:** Blockchain underpins Web3, ensuring transparent and tamper-resistant transactions.

2. Digital Identity and Privacy

2.1. **Digital Identity and Privacy:** Web3 places a premium on digital identity and privacy.

2.2. **Self-Sovereign Identity:** Users control their digital identities, reducing reliance on third-party identity providers.

2.3. **Privacy-Preserving Technologies:** Zero-knowledge proofs and other privacy technologies safeguard personal data.

2.4. **Data Monetization:** Users have the option to monetize their own data, deciding who can access it and under what conditions.

3. Decentralized Applications (DApps)

3.1. **Decentralized Applications (DApps):** DApps are at the heart of Web3, offering a new approach to software development and usage.

3.2. **Smart Contracts:** DApps use smart contracts to automate transactions, enabling trustless interactions.

3.3. **Open Ecosystem:** Developers can create and deploy DApps in an open and permissionless ecosystem.

3.4. **Interoperability:** The interoperability of DApps fosters an interconnected, decentralized internet.

4. **Cryptocurrencies and Tokenization**

4.1. **Cryptocurrencies and Tokenization:** Web3 integrates cryptocurrencies and tokenization, changing the way value is exchanged and created.

4.2. **Crypto Economies:** Cryptocurrencies are used within DApps to create new economic models, such as non-fungible tokens (NFTs) for digital assets.

4.3. **Tokenized Assets:** Traditional assets, from real estate to art, are being tokenized, enhancing liquidity and accessibility.

4.4. **Digital Collectibles:** NFTs enable the ownership of unique digital assets, from art to virtual real estate.

5. **Content Creation and Ownership**

5.1. **Content Creation and Ownership:** Web3 challenges traditional content creation and distribution models.

5.2. **Decentralized Content Platforms:** Platforms built on Web3 principles enable creators to distribute content without middlemen.

5.3. **Direct Monetization:** Creators can directly monetize their work, forging stronger relationships with their audiences.

5.4. **Immutable Provenance:** Blockchain technology ensures content ownership and provenance, combatting piracy.

6. **Challenges and Considerations**

6.1. **Challenges and Considerations:** While Web3 offers a promising vision of the future internet, it faces various challenges and considerations.

6.2. **Scalability:** Ensuring that Web3 networks can handle a high volume of users and transactions is a significant challenge.

6.3. **Regulation and Compliance:** The regulatory landscape for cryptocurrencies and decentralized technologies is evolving, posing challenges for compliance.

6.4. **User Adoption:** Encouraging mainstream user adoption of Web3 technologies is essential for its success.

Web3 represents a pivotal shift in the internet's evolution, redefining the relationship between users, technology, and information. Its emphasis on decentralization, digital identity, and user empowerment holds the potential to redefine online interactions and services in ways we're only beginning to comprehend. The future of the internet is undergoing a significant transformation, with Web3 at its forefront, offering opportunities for innovation, autonomy, and the reshaping of digital societies.

BIOMETRIC SECURITY: PROTECTING THE DIGITAL WORLD

As our digital lives become increasingly intertwined with technology, securing access to our online accounts, devices, and sensitive data is paramount. Biometric security has emerged as a powerful tool in the fight against cyber threats, offering a new level of protection based on unique physical and behavioural characteristics. In this section, we'll delve into the world of biometric security, exploring its applications, challenges, and the role it plays in safeguarding the digital landscape.

1. The Biometric Revolution

1.1. **The Biometric Revolution:** Biometrics is transforming how we authenticate our identities and protect digital assets.

1.2. **Physical and Behavioural Traits:** Biometrics relies on unique physical attributes like fingerprints and facial features, as well as behavioural characteristics like typing patterns and voice recognition.

1.3. **End of Passwords:** Biometrics represents a shift away from traditional password-based security, enhancing convenience and security.

1.4. **Multi-Modal Biometrics:** Combining multiple biometric modalities provides a robust and layered approach to security.

2. Biometric Authentication

2.1. **Biometric Authentication:** Biometric authentication is being widely adopted in various applications.

2.2. **Mobile Devices:** Smartphones use fingerprint recognition, facial recognition, and even iris scans to unlock devices and secure data.

2.3. **Physical Access Control:** Biometrics control access to secure locations, replacing key cards and PINs with fingerprint or facial recognition.

2.4. **E-commerce:** Online payment platforms use biometric authentication to verify transactions and protect financial data.

3. Advantages of Biometric Security

3.1. **Advantages of Biometric Security:** Biometric security offers several benefits over traditional authentication methods.

3.2. **Uniqueness:** Biometric traits are highly unique, making it extremely difficult for impostors to replicate.

3.3. **Convenience:** Biometrics are convenient and require no memorization of passwords.

3.4. **Non-Transferable**: Biometric data is non-transferable; an image or recording of a biometric trait cannot be used for authentication.

4. Challenges and Ethical Considerations

4.1. **Challenges and Ethical Considerations:** While biometric security offers significant advantages, it also presents challenges and ethical dilemmas.

4.2. **Privacy:** The collection and storage of biometric data raise privacy concerns, requiring robust safeguards.

4.3. **Data Protection:** Biometric data must be securely stored and encrypted to protect against data breaches.

4.4. **Ethical Use:** Ensuring the ethical use of biometrics, with transparency and consent, is vital.

5. The Future of Biometrics

5.1. **The Future of Biometrics:** The future of biometrics is brimming with possibilities.

5.2. **Continuous Authentication:** Biometric technology is moving towards continuous, real-time authentication to enhance security.

5.3. **Liveness Detection:** Advanced biometric systems incorporate liveness detection to differentiate between live individuals and spoofing attempts.

5.4. **Biometric Wearables:** Wearable devices with biometric sensors are expanding the range of applications for biometric security.

Biometric security is rapidly becoming an integral part of our digital world, enhancing security and convenience across various domains. As we navigate the challenges and ethical considerations that come with biometrics, we also stand at the cusp of a future where our unique physical and behavioural traits will serve as keys to the digital kingdom, ensuring our online experiences remain safe and secure. Biometric security is not just the present; it's the future of digital protection.

THE EVOLUTION OF IT SUPPORT AND HELPDESK ROLES

IT support and helpdesk roles have undergone a remarkable transformation as technology has advanced. What was once a primarily reactive function has evolved into a proactive and multifaceted domain. In this section, we'll explore the changing landscape of IT support and helpdesk roles, from their historical origins to their current and future state in the digital era.

1. Historical Roots

1.1. **Historical Roots:** IT support and helpdesk roles have their roots in the early days of computing.

1.2. **Break-Fix Model:** In the past, IT support primarily followed a break-fix model, where professionals responded to issues and resolved them as they arose.

1.3. **Hardware-Centric:** Early IT support was predominantly hardware-centric, focusing on fixing physical components like computers and printers.

1.4. **Localized Support:** Support teams often served a specific location or office, limiting their scope of operation.

2. The Digital Revolution

2.1. **The Digital Revolution:** The advent of personal computing and digitalization led to significant changes in IT support.

2.2. **Software Integration:** As software became central to business operations, IT support expanded to encompass software-related issues.

2.3. **Remote Support:** Advances in remote access technology allowed support teams to troubleshoot issues from a distance.

2.4. **Growing Complexity:** With the proliferation of technology, support roles became more complex and multifaceted.

3. Proactive Support

3.1. **Proactive Support:** The digital era ushered in a shift from reactive to proactive support.

3.2. **Monitoring and Maintenance:** IT support teams began proactively monitoring systems and performing routine maintenance to prevent issues.

3.3. **Predictive Analytics:** Predictive analytics and artificial intelligence (AI) are now used to forecast and prevent potential problems.

3.4. **User Training:** Educating users to prevent common issues became a part of proactive support.

4. Helpdesk as a Service

4.1. **Helpdesk as a Service:** Outsourcing and cloud-based solutions have transformed how helpdesk services are delivered.

4.2. **Cloud-Based Helpdesks:** Many organizations now use cloud-based helpdesk solutions that offer flexibility and scalability.

4.3. **Outsourcing:** Managed service providers offer outsourced helpdesk services, enabling organizations to focus on their core competencies.

4.4. **24/7 Support:** With global operations, helpdesk support often operates 24/7 to accommodate different time zones.

5. Evolving Skill Sets

5.1. **Evolving Skill Sets:** The skill sets required for IT support and helpdesk roles have evolved significantly.

5.2. **Technical Proficiency:** Professionals need in-depth knowledge of both hardware and software, as well as networking and security.

5.3. **Soft Skills:** Communication and problem-solving skills are increasingly important as support roles involve interacting with end-users.

5.4. **Adaptability:** The ability to learn and adapt to new technologies and tools is a fundamental requirement.

6. The Future of IT Support and Helpdesk Roles

6.1. The Future of IT Support and Helpdesk Roles: The future holds even more changes and opportunities for IT support and helpdesk roles.

6.2. **AI and Automation:** AI-driven chatbots and automation will play a more prominent role in support services, handling routine tasks.

6.3. **Cybersecurity:** With the increasing focus on security, support roles will involve stronger cybersecurity measures.

6.4. **Knowledge Management:** Knowledge bases and AI-powered self-service tools will be pivotal for support teams and end-users.

IT support and helpdesk roles have transformed from being purely reactive to encompassing proactive and preventative functions. As technology continues to advance, these roles will become more closely intertwined with AI and automation, offering increasingly sophisticated and efficient solutions. The evolution of IT support is a testament to the adaptability and growth of the field, ensuring that it remains an integral part of the digital age.

DATA SCIENTISTS AND THE POWER OF BIG DATA

Data science has emerged as a transformative field that harnesses the potential of big data to uncover valuable insights, drive innovation, and make data-driven decisions. In this section, we'll explore the role of data scientists, the significance of big data, and the impact this dynamic field has on various industries and domains.

1. The Rise of Data Science

1.1. **The Rise of Data Science:** Data science has emerged as a multidisciplinary field that combines statistical analysis, programming, and domain knowledge.

1.2. **Multidisciplinary Skill Set:** Data scientists possess skills in mathematics, statistics, programming, data visualization, and domain expertise.

1.3. **Data Exploration:** They explore, clean, and pre-process data, preparing it for analysis.

1.4. **Machine Learning and AI:** Data scientists use machine learning and artificial intelligence (AI) to extract insights and make predictions.

2. The Significance of Big Data

2.1. **The Significance of Big Data:** Big data represents a vast and complex landscape of information that can be harnessed for decision-making.

2.2. **Volume:** Big data encompasses massive datasets that cannot be effectively processed using traditional methods.

2.3. **Variety:** Data comes in various forms, including structured, unstructured, and semi-structured data from diverse sources.

2.4. **Velocity:** Data is generated at high speeds, often requiring real-time analysis.

3. Impact on Industries

3.1. **Impact on Industries:** Data science and big data are reshaping various industries and sectors.

3.2. **Healthcare:** Predictive analytics and electronic health records are transforming patient care.

3.3. **Finance:** Data science is used in algorithmic trading, fraud detection, and risk management.

3.4. **Retail:** Big data is leveraged for customer analytics, demand forecasting, and inventory optimization.

3.5. **Transportation:** Data is used for route optimization, autonomous vehicles, and predictive maintenance.

4. Ethical Considerations

4.1. **Ethical Considerations:** The power of data science and big data also raises ethical concerns.

4.2. **Data Privacy:** Protecting the privacy of individuals' data is a paramount concern.

4.3. **Bias and Fairness:** Ensuring that data and algorithms are unbiased and fair is critical.

4.4. **Transparency:** Transparent use of data and algorithms is essential for trust.

5. The Future of Data Science

5.1. **The Future of Data Science:** Data science is an ever-evolving field with a promising future.

5.2. **Edge Computing:** Data science will extend to edge computing, enabling real-time analysis at the source of data generation.

5.3. **Explainable AI:** Explainable AI is vital for making machine learning models more transparent and interpretable.

5.4. **Responsible AI:** A focus on responsible AI involves ethical development, deployment, and monitoring of AI systems.

Data scientists are at the forefront of the big data revolution, uncovering hidden insights, guiding decision-making, and driving innovation across various domains. As the data landscape continues to expand, the impact of data science on our world will only grow, creating new opportunities and challenges. The power of big data, harnessed by skilled data scientists, is shaping the future of innovation and progress.

CYBERSECURITY EXPERTS: GUARDIANS OF THE DIGITAL REALM

In an increasingly interconnected and digitally dependent world, the role of cybersecurity experts has never been more critical. These professionals are tasked with protecting digital assets, sensitive information, and the integrity of online systems. In this section, we'll explore the world of cybersecurity experts, the evolving threat landscape, and the pivotal role they play in safeguarding the digital realm.

1. The Rise of Cybersecurity

1.1. **The Rise of Cybersecurity:** The digital revolution brought with it a new era of cybersecurity challenges and opportunities.

1.2. **Proliferation of Data:** As digital data exploded in volume, protecting it became a top priority.

1.3. **Evolving Threat Landscape:** Threat actors continuously develop new tactics, techniques, and procedures (TTPs), requiring cybersecurity experts to adapt and innovate.

1.4. **Cybersecurity Frameworks:** The adoption of cybersecurity frameworks and standards became essential for effective defense.

2. The Role of Cybersecurity Experts

2.1. **The Role of Cybersecurity Experts:** Cybersecurity experts play a multifaceted role in defending against cyber threats.

2.2. **Risk Assessment:** They assess vulnerabilities, threats, and the potential impact of security breaches.

2.3. **Incident Response:** Cybersecurity experts are the first responders in the event of a security incident, mitigating damage and restoring normal operations.

2.4. **Security Architecture:** They design and implement security systems, firewalls, and encryption to protect against threats.

3. The Threat Landscape

3.1. **The Threat Landscape:** Cybersecurity experts face a wide range of threats in their battle to secure digital assets.

3.2. **Malware:** Malicious software, including viruses, ransomware, and spyware, threatens data integrity and privacy.

3.3. **Phishing and Social Engineering:** Deceptive tactics manipulate individuals into revealing sensitive information.

3.4. **Advanced Persistent Threats (APTs):** APTs are sophisticated, long-term cyberattacks often associated with nation-states or organized crime.

4. Ethical and Legal Considerations

4.1. **Ethical and Legal Considerations:** Cybersecurity experts must navigate complex ethical and legal landscapes.

4.2. **Ethical Hacking:** Ethical hackers, or "white hat" hackers, use their skills to identify vulnerabilities and weaknesses, assisting in strengthening security.

4.3. **Compliance and Regulations:** Staying compliant with legal and industry-specific regulations is crucial for cybersecurity experts.

4.4. **Data Privacy:** Safeguarding user data and privacy has become a top priority with the introduction of GDPR and other privacy laws.

5. The Future of Cybersecurity

5.1. **The Future of Cybersecurity:** The field of cybersecurity is poised for continued growth and evolution.

5.2. **AI and Automation:** Artificial intelligence and automation are increasingly used for threat detection and response.

5.3. **Cloud Security:** As organizations transition to the cloud, securing cloud environments becomes a focus for cybersecurity experts.

5.4. **Zero Trust Architecture:** The adoption of a zero-trust model emphasizes strict access controls and continuous monitoring.

Cybersecurity experts are the unsung heroes of the digital age, tirelessly working behind the scenes to protect our digital world from an ever-evolving array of threats. As technology continues to advance, their role in safeguarding the digital realm remains indispensable. In a world where the next cyber threat is always around the corner, cybersecurity experts stand as the guardians of our digital future.

DEVOPS ENGINEERS: BRIDGING THE GAP BETWEEN DEVELOPMENT AND OPERATIONS

DevOps engineers are at the forefront of a transformative movement that aims to streamline software development and delivery by bridging the traditional gap between development and IT operations. In this section, we'll explore the pivotal role of DevOps engineers, the principles of DevOps, and their impact on the world of software development and IT operations.

1. The Birth of DevOps

1.1. **The Birth of DevOps:** DevOps is a response to the siloed nature of traditional software development and IT operations.

1.2. **Siloed Departments:** In the past, development and operations teams often worked in isolation, leading to inefficiencies and communication challenges.

1.3. **Continuous Integration and Continuous Deployment (CI/CD):** DevOps promotes a CI/CD pipeline for automated software delivery and deployment.

1.4. **Agile and Lean Principles:** DevOps draws inspiration from agile and lean methodologies to streamline processes.

1.5. **The Role of DevOps Engineers**

1.6. **The Role of DevOps Engineers:** DevOps engineers play a pivotal role in bridging the gap between development and operations.

1.7. **Automation:** They automate repetitive tasks, such as software builds, testing, and deployments.

1.8. **Collaboration:** DevOps engineers facilitate collaboration and communication between development and operations teams.

1.9. **Monitoring and Feedback:** They implement monitoring tools to provide feedback on the performance and stability of software in production.

2. **Key DevOps Principles**

2.1. **Key DevOps Principles:** DevOps is guided by several key principles that govern its practices.

2.2. **Collaboration:** DevOps emphasizes a culture of collaboration and shared responsibility among teams.

2.3. **Automation:** Automation is fundamental to reducing manual and error-prone processes.

2.4. **Feedback Loop:** A strong feedback loop is crucial for continuous improvement and adaptation.

3. Impact on Software Development

3.1. **Impact on Software Development:** DevOps has revolutionized the software development lifecycle.

3.2. **Faster Release Cycles:** DevOps shortens release cycles, enabling rapid feature delivery.

3.3. **Improved Quality:** Continuous testing and automated deployment contribute to higher software quality.

3.4. **Enhanced Flexibility:** The ability to roll out incremental updates improves the flexibility to respond to changing requirements.

4. Impact on IT Operations

4.1. **Impact on IT Operations:** DevOps also transforms the landscape of IT operations.

4.2. **Scalability:** Operations teams are equipped to scale infrastructure dynamically to accommodate changing workloads.

4.3. **Infrastructure as Code (IaC):** IaC allows the management of infrastructure through code, improving consistency and repeatability.

4.4. **Resilience and Stability:** DevOps practices enhance system resilience and stability through automation and monitoring.

5. The Future of DevOps

5.1. **The Future of DevOps:** DevOps is poised for continued growth and evolution.

5.2. **Security:** Integrating security into the DevOps process, known as DevSecOps, is becoming increasingly important.

5.3. **Serverless and Cloud-Native:** DevOps practices are evolving to accommodate serverless and cloud-native architectures.

5.4. **AIOps:** Artificial intelligence and machine learning are being used to enhance operations and automate incident response.

DevOps engineers are the architects of a cultural and technological revolution, transforming the way software is developed, deployed, and managed. Their role in bridging the divide between development and operations is crucial to delivering value to end-users quickly and efficiently. As DevOps continues to evolve and integrate new technologies, it remains a driving force in the world of software development and IT operations.

UX/UI DESIGNERS: CRAFTING USER-CENTRIC EXPERIENCES

User Experience (UX) and User Interface (UI) designers are central to the creation of digital products and services that resonate with users. They are responsible for ensuring that the interfaces are not only visually appealing but also functional and user-friendly. In this section, we'll delve into the pivotal role of UX/UI designers, their processes, and the impact of their work on the digital world.

1. The Evolution of User-Centric Design

1.1. **The Evolution of User-Centric Design:** User-centric design has grown in importance with the rise of digital products.

1.2. **Early Interfaces:** In the past, user interfaces were often rudimentary and less focused on user experience.

1.3. **The Human-Computer Interaction Field:** The HCI field laid the foundation for user-cantered design principles.

1.4. **Rise of Digital Products:** The proliferation of digital products heightened the importance of UX/UI design.

2. The Role of UX/UI Designers

2.1. **The Role of UX/UI Designers:** UX/UI designers are responsible for creating user-cantered digital interfaces.

2.2. **User Research:** They conduct user research to understand the needs and preferences of their target audience.

2.3. **Information Architecture:** UX/UI designers structure information to ensure efficient navigation and information retrieval.

2.4. **Visual Design:** They craft the visual elements, including layouts, colour schemes, and typography.

3. Key Principles of User-Centric Design

3.1. **Key Principles of User-Centric Design:** UX/UI designers adhere to several fundamental principles.

3.2. **Usability:** Interfaces must be easy to use and intuitive.

3.3. **Accessibility:** Ensuring that digital products are accessible to users with disabilities.

3.4. **Consistency:** Consistent design elements create a familiar and comfortable experience.

4. Impact on Digital Products

Impact on Digital Products: The work of UX/UI designers directly influences the success of digital products.

4.1.1.**User Satisfaction:** Well-designed products lead to higher user satisfaction and retention.

4.1.2.**Conversion Rates:** E-commerce platforms benefit from improved conversion rates through better user experiences.

4.1.3.**Brand Reputation:** A positive digital experience enhances brand reputation and user loyalty.

5. The Design Process

5.1. **The Design Process**: UX/UI designers follow a structured design process.

5.2. **Research:** This phase involves understanding the target audience, their needs, and the problem space.

5.3. **Design:** Designers create wireframes and prototypes to visualize the product's structure and flow.

5.4. **Testing and Iteration:** Prototypes are tested with users, and feedback is used to make improvements.

6. The Future of UX/UI Design

6.1. **The Future of UX/UI Design:** The field of UX/UI design is constantly evolving.

6.2. **Voice and Gesture Interfaces:** Designers are adapting to the rise of voice and gesture interfaces.

6.3. **Data-Driven Design:** Data analysis is used to inform design decisions and personalize user experiences.

6.4. **Augmented and Virtual Reality:** UX/UI designers are exploring the unique challenges and opportunities presented by AR and VR interfaces.

UX/UI designers play a pivotal role in shaping the digital landscape, ensuring that users have meaningful and enjoyable experiences with digital products. As technology continues to advance, their role in creating user-centric designs remains essential for the success of digital products and services. UX/UI designers are at the forefront of creating the digital experiences that define our digital world.

DIGITAL MARKETING IN THE AGE OF PERSONALIZATION

The digital marketing landscape has evolved significantly with the advent of personalization. Today, successful marketing goes beyond generic advertisements and appeals to individual preferences and behaviors. In this section, we'll explore the role of personalization in digital marketing, the technologies that make it possible, and its impact on brands and consumers.

1. The Era of Personalization

1.1. **The Era of Personalization:** Personalization in digital marketing is a response to changing consumer expectations.

1.2. **The Shift from Mass Marketing:** Traditional mass marketing is giving way to personalized experiences.

1.3. **Consumer Empowerment:** Consumers expect relevant content and offers tailored to their interests.

1.4. **Data-Driven Insights:** Data analytics and technology have made personalization feasible.

2. The Role of Personalization

2.1. The Role of Personalization: Personalization enhances the effectiveness of digital marketing efforts.

2.2. Content Customization: Tailoring content to individual preferences increases engagement and conversion rates.

2.3. Product Recommendations: E-commerce platforms use recommendation engines to suggest products based on user behavior.

2.4. Email Marketing: Personalized email marketing campaigns yield higher open and click-through rates.

3. Technologies and Tools

3.1. Technologies and Tools: Various technologies enable personalization in digital marketing.

3.2. Artificial Intelligence (AI): AI algorithms analyse data to make personalized content recommendations.

3.3. Machine Learning: ML algorithms continuously adapt to user behavior, refining recommendations over time.

3.4. **Customer Relationship Management (CRM):** CRM software stores and manages customer data for personalized marketing campaigns.

4. The Impact on Brands

4.1. **The Impact on Brands:** Personalization benefits brands in several ways.

4.2. **Improved Customer Loyalty:** Personalized experiences create stronger bonds with customers.

4.3. **Higher Conversion Rates:** Relevance leads to better conversion rates and increased sales.

4.4. **Data-Driven Decision Making:** Brands can make data-informed decisions and adapt to changing consumer preferences.

5. The Impact on Consumers

5.1.1. **The Impact on Consumers:** Consumers also benefit from personalized marketing.

5.1.2. **Relevant Content:** Personalization ensures that consumers receive content and offers relevant to their interests.

5.1.3. **Time Efficiency:** Consumers are presented with products or information that they are more likely to engage with.

5.1.4. **Enhanced Shopping Experience:** Personalized shopping experiences make online navigation more enjoyable.

6. Ethical Considerations

6.1. **Ethical Considerations:** While personalization offers many benefits, it also raises ethical concerns.

6.2. **Data Privacy:** The collection and use of personal data must adhere to privacy regulations and respect user consent.

6.3. **Transparency:** Brands must be transparent about data usage and inform users about personalization practices.

6.4. **Bias Mitigation:** Efforts must be made to avoid algorithmic bias and ensure fair personalization.

Personalization in digital marketing is a powerful tool for brands to connect with their audience on a deeper level. By offering relevant content and products, brands can enhance customer satisfaction and loyalty. However, it's essential for brands to handle personal data ethically and transparently. As technology continues to advance, personalization will remain a cornerstone of successful digital marketing strategies, delivering value to both brands and consumers in the age of personalization.

REMOTE WORK AND THE GIG ECONOMY

Remote work and the gig economy have transformed the traditional employment landscape. These trends have given rise to new opportunities for workers and new challenges for organizations. In this section, we'll explore the growing prevalence of remote work and the gig economy, their impact on both employers and workers, and the future of work in a digitally connected world.

1. The Rise of Remote Work

1.1. **The Rise of Remote Work:** The digital age has made remote work more accessible and prevalent.

1.2. **Technological Advancements:** High-speed internet, cloud computing, and collaboration tools have enabled remote work.

1.3. **Flexibility:** Remote work offers employees the flexibility to choose their work environment and hours.

1.4. **Global Talent Pool:** Employers can tap into a global talent pool, transcending geographic limitations.

2. Benefits and Challenges

2.1. **Benefits and Challenges:** Remote work offers various advantages but also presents unique challenges.

2.2. **Advantages:** Reduced commuting time, increased work-life balance, and access to a broader talent pool.

2.3. **Challenges:** Potential feelings of isolation, difficulties in communication, and the need for self-discipline.

2.4. **Hybrid Models:** Many organizations are adopting hybrid work models, allowing employees to work both in the office and remotely.

3. The Gig Economy

3.1. **The Gig Economy:** The gig economy encompasses a workforce of independent contractors and freelancers.

3.2. **Independence**: Gig workers have the flexibility to choose their projects and clients.

3.3. **Diverse Skillsets:** The gig economy accommodates a wide range of skills, from gig economy drivers to freelance designers and writers.

3.4. **Challenges:** Gig workers face income volatility and may not have access to traditional employment benefits.

4. Impact on Employers

4.1. **Impact on Employers:** Organizations are adapting to remote work and the gig economy.

4.2. **Cost Savings:** Remote work can lead to reduced office space costs and overhead.

4.3. **Access to Diverse Talent:** Employers can access specialized skills from across the globe through gig workers.

4.4. **Management Challenges:** Managing remote teams and gig workers requires effective communication and project management.

5. Impact on Workers

5.1. **Impact on Workers:** Both remote work and the gig economy offer new opportunities and challenges for workers.

5.2. **Work-Life Balance:** Remote work can enhance work-life balance, but it may also blur the boundaries between work and personal life.

5.3. **Income Stability:** Gig workers may experience income variability, making financial planning more complex.

5.4. **Skill Development:** Remote workers often develop self-discipline and time management skills, while gig workers gain diverse experiences.

6. The Future of Work

6.1. **The Future of Work:** The future of work is likely to be characterized by continued growth in remote work and gig employment.

6.2. **Workforce Flexibility:** Remote work and the gig economy offer workforce flexibility, allowing individuals to craft their careers to better suit their needs.

6.3. **Regulation and Benefits:** Policymakers and businesses are grappling with how to regulate and provide benefits to gig workers.

6.4. **Digital Transformation:** The ongoing digital transformation will continue to enable remote work and facilitate the gig economy.

Remote work and the gig economy have altered the employment landscape, offering both workers and organizations new possibilities. As technology and communication tools continue to advance, these trends are likely to remain a significant force in the future of work, reshaping traditional employment structures and giving individuals greater control over their careers.

TECH-ENABLED HEALTHCARE: THE ROLE OF TELEMEDICINE

Telemedicine is revolutionizing healthcare by leveraging technology to deliver medical services remotely. In this section, we'll explore the growth of telemedicine, its impact on patient care and the healthcare industry, and the promise it holds for the future of healthcare.

1. The Rise of Telemedicine

1.1. **The Rise of Telemedicine:** Telemedicine has witnessed a significant surge in adoption due to technological advancements.

1.2. **Technological Enablers:** High-speed internet, mobile devices, and telehealth platforms have made remote consultations possible.

1.3. **Healthcare Access:** Telemedicine extends healthcare access to remote and underserved areas.

1.4. **Pandemic Response:** The COVID-19 pandemic accelerated the adoption of telemedicine as a safer way to provide care.

3. The Role of Telemedicine

3.1. **The Role of Telemedicine:** Telemedicine serves a multitude of purposes in the healthcare ecosystem.

3.2. **Remote Consultations:** Patients can consult with healthcare providers via video calls, phone calls, or chat for non-emergency medical issues.

3.3. **Specialist Consultations:** Telemedicine facilitates access to specialists, even in areas where they are scarce.

3.4. **Chronic Disease Management:** Patients with chronic conditions can receive ongoing care and monitoring through telehealth.

4. Advantages of Telemedicine

4.1. **Advantages of Telemedicine:** Telemedicine offers several benefits for both patients and healthcare providers.

4.2. **Convenience:** Patients can receive care from the comfort of their homes, eliminating travel and waiting times.

4.3. **Access to Specialists:** Telemedicine allows for timely consultations with specialists.

4.4. **Reduced Healthcare Costs:** Fewer in-person visits can result in cost savings for both patients and healthcare systems.

5. Challenges and Considerations

5.1. **Challenges and Considerations:** Despite its advantages, telemedicine also faces challenges.

5.2. **Digital Divide:** Not all patients have access to the necessary technology, creating disparities in healthcare access.

5.3. **Regulatory and Legal Challenges:** Telemedicine regulations vary by region and require ongoing updates to ensure quality and patient safety.

5.4. **Security and Privacy:** Protecting patient data and ensuring the security of telehealth platforms are paramount.

6.   The Future of Telemedicine

6.1. **The Future of Telemedicine:** Telemedicine is poised for further growth and innovation.

6.2. **Telehealth Platforms:** Advanced platforms will offer features like remote monitoring, AI diagnostics, and integration with electronic health records.

6.3. **Hybrid Models:** Hybrid models that combine in-person and telemedicine care will become more common.

6.4. **Global Reach:** Telemedicine will extend its reach globally, linking patients with healthcare providers around the world.

Telemedicine is transforming healthcare by expanding access to medical services, improving patient convenience, and enhancing healthcare delivery. As technology continues to advance and regulatory barriers are addressed, telemedicine is likely to play an increasingly integral role in the healthcare landscape, providing a brighter and more accessible future for patients and healthcare providers alike.

SMART CITIES AND THE URBAN TECH REVOLUTION

The concept of smart cities represents a vision for the future of urban living, where technology is harnessed to enhance the quality of life for city residents, improve resource management, and address urban challenges. In this section, we'll explore the rise of smart cities, the technologies driving this urban tech revolution, and the potential impact on urban living.

1. The Emergence of Smart Cities

1.1. **The Emergence of Smart Cities:** Smart cities have emerged as a response to the challenges of urbanization and the growing demands of urban living.

1.2. **Rapid Urbanization:** Cities worldwide are experiencing population growth, placing strain on infrastructure and services.

1.3. **Technological Advancements:** Advances in technology have made it possible to build more connected and efficient urban environments.

1.4. **Sustainability:** Smart cities aim to reduce environmental impact and improve resource management.

2. Key Technologies and Components

2.1. **Key Technologies and Components:** Several technologies and components are pivotal to the development of smart cities.

2.2. **Internet of Things (IoT):** IoT sensors and devices collect data on various urban parameters, from traffic flow to air quality.

2.3. **Data Analytics:** Data analytics tools process the vast amounts of data generated to derive insights and optimize city functions.

2.4. **Connected Infrastructure:** Infrastructure elements, such as smart grids, are interconnected to manage resources efficiently.

3. Smart City Applications

3.1. **Smart City Applications:** Smart cities apply technology to various aspects of urban living.

3.2. **Transportation:** Smart transportation systems reduce traffic congestion, enhance public transit, and improve parking management.

3.3. **Energy Management:** Smart grids and energy-efficient technologies reduce energy consumption and carbon emissions.

3.4. **Public Services:** Technologies like e-governance and digital platforms improve the delivery of public services.

4. Benefits and Challenges

4.1. **Benefits and Challenges:** Smart cities offer numerous benefits, but they also come with unique challenges.

4.2. **Benefits:** Improved quality of life, resource efficiency, sustainability, and enhanced safety.

4.3. **Challenges:** Data privacy concerns, cybersecurity risks, and the need for significant infrastructure investment.

5. Sustainability and Resilience

5.1. **Sustainability and Resilience:** Smart cities focus on sustainable and resilient urban development.

5.2. **Green Infrastructure:** Sustainable architecture and urban planning prioritize green spaces and environmentally friendly designs.

5.3. **Disaster Preparedness:** Resilient smart cities are prepared for natural disasters and can respond effectively.

5.4. **Resource Efficiency:** Resource optimization reduces waste and energy consumption.

6. The Future of Smart Cities

6.1. **The Future of Smart Cities:** The growth of smart cities is expected to continue.

6.2. **5G and Connectivity:** The rollout of 5G networks will enhance connectivity and support more advanced IoT applications.

6.3. **AI and Automation:** Artificial intelligence and automation will play a greater role in optimizing urban functions.

6.4. **Urban Innovation Hubs:** Urban innovation hubs will continue to drive research and development in urban technologies.

Smart cities are a response to the complex challenges posed by urbanization and the digital age. As technology continues to advance and cities evolve, smart cities are poised to become an integral part of the urban landscape, improving the quality of life for residents, addressing resource management, and promoting sustainability and resilience in urban environments.

LEGAL TECH AND THE INTERSECTION OF LAW AND TECHNOLOGY

Legal tech represents the merging of the legal industry with cutting-edge technology, transforming the way legal professionals work, enhancing access to justice, and improving the efficiency of legal processes. In this section, we'll explore the growing field of legal tech, its impact on the legal sector, and the potential it holds for the future of law.

1. The Emergence of Legal Tech

1.1. **The Emergence of Legal Tech:** Legal tech has evolved in response to the need for more efficient and accessible legal services.

1.2. **Challenges in the Legal Industry:** The legal field faces challenges related to efficiency, access to justice, and cost.

1.3. **Advancements in Technology:** The advancement of technologies like artificial intelligence and data analytics has enabled innovation in the legal sector.

1.4. **Improved Access:** Legal tech aims to improve access to legal services for individuals and businesses.

2. Key Components and Technologies

2.1. **Key Components and Technologies:** Legal tech leverages various technologies and components.

2.2. **Artificial Intelligence (AI):** AI is used for contract analysis, legal research, and predictive analytics.

2.3. **Document Automation:** Automation tools streamline the creation of legal documents.

2.4. **Blockchain:** Blockchain is used for secure record-keeping and digital notarization.

3. Applications in the Legal Industry

3.1. **Applications in the Legal Industry:** Legal tech is applied to various aspects of legal practice.

3.2. **Legal Research:** AI-powered tools assist legal professionals in researching cases, statutes, and legal precedents.

3.3. **Document Management:** Document automation tools help generate legal documents, contracts, and agreements more efficiently.

3.4. **e-Discovery:** Electronic discovery software aids in the identification and retrieval of relevant legal information in large datasets.

4. Benefits and Challenges

4.1. **Benefits and Challenges:** Legal tech brings several advantages but also presents challenges to the legal industry.

4.2. **Efficiency:** Legal tech streamlines processes, making legal services more efficient.

4.3. **Cost Savings:** Automation and AI reduce the cost of legal services.

4.4. **Data Security:** Protecting sensitive legal data is crucial, requiring robust cybersecurity measures.

5. The Future of Legal Tech

5.1. **The Future of Legal Tech:** Legal tech is expected to continue evolving and expanding.

5.2. **Access to Justice:** Legal tech is working to bridge the justice gap by making legal services more accessible.

5.3. **Legal Analytics:** Predictive analytics and data-driven decision-making will become more prevalent in the legal industry.

5.4. **Regulatory Challenges:** The legal sector is addressing regulatory issues related to technology, such as data privacy and ethical AI use.

Legal tech is reshaping the practice of law, making it more accessible, efficient, and cost-effective. As technology continues to advance and legal professionals embrace innovative solutions, legal tech is poised to play an increasingly significant role in the legal field, enhancing legal services for individuals and organizations while addressing longstanding challenges in the justice system.

ENVIRONMENTAL TECH: SUSTAINABILITY IN THE DIGITAL AGE

Environmental technology, often referred to as "envirotech" or "cleantech," harnesses the power of digital innovations to address critical environmental challenges and promote sustainability. In this section, we'll explore the rise of environmental tech, the technologies driving this movement, and its potential to contribute to a more sustainable future.

1. The Emergence of Environmental Tech

1.1. **The Emergence of Environmental Tech:** Environmental tech has emerged as a response to pressing environmental issues and the need for innovative solutions.

1.2. **Environmental Challenges:** Climate change, resource depletion, and pollution have intensified the need for sustainable solutions.

1.3. **Digital Transformation:** The ongoing digital transformation provides tools to address environmental challenges effectively.

1.4. **Sustainable Development Goals:** Global goals like the UN's Sustainable Development Goals (SDGs) emphasize the importance of environmental sustainability.

2. Key Technologies and Components

2.1. **Key Technologies and Components:** Environmental tech leverages various technologies and components.

2.2. **Internet of Things (IoT):** IoT sensors monitor environmental conditions, collect data on energy usage, and enable smart resource management.

2.3. **Renewable Energy:** Solar, wind, and hydropower technologies generate clean energy.

2.4. **Data Analytics:** Data analytics tools process large datasets to gain insights into environmental trends and optimize resource use.

3. Applications in Environmental Tech

3.1. **Applications in Environmental Tech:** Environmental tech is applied to various aspects of environmental conservation and sustainability.

3.2. **Smart Grids:** Smart grids manage electricity distribution efficiently, reducing energy wastage.

3.3. **Waste Management:** IoT-enabled waste management systems optimize collection routes and minimize landfill use.

3.4. **Water Conservation:** Environmental tech monitors water quality, enables efficient irrigation, and promotes responsible water use.

4. Benefits and Challenges

4.1. **Benefits and Challenges:** Environmental tech offers significant benefits but also presents challenges.

4.2. **Sustainability:** Environmental tech contributes to a more sustainable future, reducing carbon emissions and resource consumption.

4.3. **Cost Savings:** Energy-efficient technologies often result in cost savings for businesses and individuals.

4.4. **Technological Barriers:** Overcoming technological and infrastructural barriers is necessary for the widespread adoption of environmental tech.

5. The Future of Environmental Tech

5.1. **The Future of Environmental Tech:** Environmental tech is poised for continued growth and innovation.

5.2. **Circular Economy:** The circular economy, which emphasizes recycling and waste reduction, will be a focus of environmental tech.

5.3. **Green Transportation:** Electric vehicles and sustainable transportation solutions will become more prominent.

5.4. **Environmental Data Platforms:** Environmental data platforms will offer insights and solutions for managing natural resources effectively.

Environmental tech represents an exciting frontier in the quest for environmental sustainability. As technology continues to advance, the potential for innovative solutions to address environmental challenges is vast. Environmental tech is not only crucial for mitigating environmental degradation but also holds the promise of creating a greener and more sustainable future for generations to come.

EDUCATION IN THE DIGITAL ERA: EDTECH AND E-LEARNING

The digital era has ushered in a transformation in education, with technology playing a central role in teaching and learning. This section explores the rise of EdTech and e-learning, the technologies powering this educational revolution, and the potential impact on the future of learning.

1. The Digital Transformation of Education

1.1. **The Digital Transformation of Education:** Education is experiencing a profound shift due to digital technology.

1.2. **Access to Information:** The internet provides instant access to vast amounts of information and educational resources.

1.3. **Global Connectivity:** Digital tools enable learners to connect with educators and peers worldwide.

1.4. **Personalization:** EdTech allows for personalized learning experiences tailored to individual needs.

2. Key Technologies and Components

2.1. **Key Technologies and Components:** Educational technology leverages various technologies and components.

2.2. **Learning Management Systems (LMS):** LMS platforms facilitate course management, content delivery, and assessment.

2.3. **Virtual Reality (VR) and Augmented Reality (AR):** These technologies enhance immersive learning experiences.

2.4. **Artificial Intelligence (AI):** AI assists in personalized content recommendations and adaptive learning.

3. Applications in EdTech and E-Learning

3.1. **Applications in EdTech and E-Learning:** Digital education encompasses various aspects of learning.

3.2. **Online Learning Platforms:** EdTech platforms provide a wide range of online courses and degrees.

3.3. **Blended Learning:** Combining in-person and online teaching methods enhances flexibility.

3.4. **Gamification:** Gamified learning engages students and encourages participation.

4. Benefits and Challenges

4.1. **Benefits and Challenges:** EdTech and e-learning offer numerous advantages but also come with challenges.

4.2. **Accessibility:** Digital education makes learning accessible to a global audience.

4.3. **Cost-Effective:** Online education often reduces the cost of traditional classroom-based learning.

4.4. **Digital Divide:** Bridging the digital divide is crucial to ensure equitable access to educational resources.

5. The Future of EdTech and E-Learning

5.1. **The Future of EdTech and E-Learning:** The future of education is closely tied to technology.

5.2. **Hybrid Models:** Hybrid learning models combining in-person and online elements are expected to become more common.

5.3. **AI-Powered Learning:** AI-driven platforms will offer more personalized and adaptive learning experiences.

5.4. **Global Learning Networks:** Technology will continue to connect learners and educators from around the world.

Education in the digital era is evolving to provide learners with unprecedented opportunities for flexibility, personalization, and access to knowledge. As technology advances, the potential to transform traditional educational models and deliver a more inclusive and tailored learning experience becomes increasingly tangible. EdTech and e-learning are at the forefront of this educational revolution, shaping the future of learning for students of all ages and backgrounds.

PREPARING FOR THE UNPREDICTABLE: LIFELONG LEARNING AND SKILL BUILDING

In an era of constant change and technological advancement, the need for continuous learning and skill development is paramount. This section explores the importance of lifelong learning, strategies for skill building, and the evolving landscape of education and training.

1. The Imperative of Lifelong Learning

The Imperative of Lifelong Learning: The pace of change in the digital age necessitates ongoing learning.

1.1. **The Evolving Work Landscape:** Jobs and industries are constantly evolving, demanding new skills and knowledge.

1.2. **Adapting to Technology:** Technology is an integral part of daily life, and keeping up with it is essential.

1.3. **Personal and Professional Growth:** Lifelong learning enhances personal development and career advancement.

2. Strategies for Lifelong Learning

2.1. **Strategies for Lifelong Learning:** Embracing lifelong learning requires a strategic approach.

2.2. **Online Learning Platforms:** Platforms like Coursera, edX, and LinkedIn Learning offer a wide range of courses.

2.3. **Microlearning:** Short, focused lessons make it easier to acquire new skills in bite-sized portions.

2.4. **Networking and Mentorship:** Connecting with peers and mentors can provide valuable insights and learning opportunities.

3. The Role of Upskilling and Reskilling

3.1. **The Role of Upskilling and Reskilling:** Upskilling and reskilling are essential in a changing job market.

3.2. **Upskilling:** Enhancing existing skills or learning new skills to stay relevant in your current field.

3.3. **Reskilling:** Learning entirely new skills to transition into a different career or industry.

3.4. **Government and Corporate Initiatives:** Many organizations and governments are investing in upskilling and reskilling programs.

4. Self-Directed Learning

4.1. **Self-Directed Learning:** Taking charge of your learning journey is a key aspect of lifelong learning.

4.2. **Curiosity and Self-Motivation:** Cultivating curiosity and self-motivation are crucial for self-directed learning.

4.3. **Setting Goals:** Clearly defined goals help structure your learning path.

4.4. **Experimentation and Continuous Assessment:** Experimenting with different learning approaches and continuously assessing progress are essential.

5. The Evolving Landscape of Education

5.1. **The Evolving Landscape of Education:** Traditional education is adapting to the demands of lifelong learning.

5.2. **Online Degrees and Certificates:** Institutions offer online programs for degree completion and certification.

5.3. **Open Educational Resources (OER):** OER provides free or low-cost educational materials, textbooks, and courses.

5.4. **Micro credentials and Badges:** Short courses and digital badges recognize specific skills and competencies.

6. Preparing for the Future

6.1. **Preparing for the Future:** Lifelong learning is not only about the present; it's also about future-proofing yourself.

6.2. **Anticipating Industry Trends:** Stay informed about industry trends and emerging technologies.

6.3. **Adaptability and Resilience:** Being adaptable and resilient in the face of change is a valuable skill.

6.4. **Balance of Hard and Soft Skills:** Develop a balance of hard skills (technical) and soft skills (communication, leadership).

Lifelong learning and skill building are the keys to navigating a rapidly changing world. Whether you're looking to stay competitive in your current job, transition to a new career, or simply expand your horizons, embracing the mindset of a lifelong learner will empower you to thrive in an unpredictable future.

NETWORKING AND BUILDING YOUR PERSONAL BRAND

In the digital age, personal branding and effective networking are essential skills for personal and professional success. This section explores the importance of networking, strategies for building your personal brand, and the ways in which technology and online platforms play a crucial role in these endeavours.

1. The Power of Networking

1.1. **The Power of Networking:** Networking is a valuable tool for personal and professional growth.

1.2. **Expanding Opportunities:** Networking opens doors to new opportunities, whether it's finding a job, collaborating on a project, or seeking mentorship.

1.3. **Building Relationships:** Building strong professional relationships can lead to long-term partnerships and collaborations.

1.4. **Learning and Sharing Knowledge:** Networking allows you to learn from others, share your expertise, and stay informed about industry trends.

2. Strategies for Effective Networking

2.1. **Strategies for Effective Networking:** Successful networking requires a deliberate approach.

2.2. **Online and In-Person Networking:** Utilize both online platforms and in-person events to expand your network.

2.3. **LinkedIn and social media:** Platforms like LinkedIn, Twitter, and Instagram are valuable for connecting with professionals and sharing your expertise.

2.4. **Professional Organizations:** Joining industry-specific associations and attending conferences can enhance your network.

3. Building Your Personal Brand

Building Your Personal Brand: Your personal brand is how you present yourself to the world, and it plays a critical role in networking.

Defining Your Brand: Identify your unique strengths, values, and what you want to be known for.

Consistency: Consistency in your online presence and interactions helps build a strong personal brand.

Content Creation: Sharing valuable content, whether through blogging, social media, or other channels, reinforces your brand.

4. Leveraging Technology

4.1. **Leveraging Technology:** Technology plays a significant role in personal branding and networking.

4.2. **Online Portfolios:** Creating a personal website or portfolio can showcase your skills and expertise.

4.3. **Content Creation Tools:** Utilize tools for content creation, such as Canva, for professional graphics and visuals.

4.4. **Virtual Networking Events:** Attend virtual networking events, webinars, and conferences to expand your network.

5. Cultivating a Digital Presence

5.1. **Cultivating a Digital Presence:** Your online presence is an extension of your personal brand.

5.2. **Engage with Your Audience:** Respond to comments, participate in discussions, and engage with your online audience.

5.3. **Professional Headshot:** Use a professional headshot for your online profiles to convey a polished image.

5.4. **Regular Updates:** Keep your profiles up to date with your latest accomplishments, skills, and projects.

6. Measuring Your Impact

6.1. **Measuring Your Impact:** It's important to assess the effectiveness of your personal brand and networking efforts.

6.2. **Analytics and Metrics:** Use analytics tools to track the performance of your online content and networking activities.

6.3. **Feedback and Self-Reflection:** Seek feedback from your network and reflect on how you can improve your personal brand and networking strategies.

6.4. **Adjust and Adapt:** Be willing to adjust your strategies as needed to achieve your personal and professional goals.

Networking and personal branding are instrumental in achieving personal and professional success in the digital age. By strategically building your personal brand and utilizing technology to expand your network, you can create valuable opportunities, foster meaningful connections, and distinguish yourself in your field. Cultivating a strong personal brand and network will help you thrive in an increasingly interconnected and competitive world.

NAVIGATING TECH JOB INTERVIEWS AND RESUMES

Securing a tech job in the digital age requires not only the right skills but also a well-crafted resume and effective interview strategies. In this section, we'll explore the key components of a tech resume, offer tips for interview success, and provide insights into the evolving nature of tech job interviews.

1. Crafting an Effective Tech Resume

1.1. **Crafting an Effective Tech Resume:** Your resume is your first impression on potential employers, so it's essential to make it impactful.

1.2. **Highlighting Technical Skills:** Clearly list your technical skills and technologies you're proficient in.

1.3. **Quantifying Achievements:** Use numbers and metrics to quantify your accomplishments and contributions in previous roles.

1.4. **Tailoring to the Job:** Customize your resume for each job application to match the specific job requirements.

2. The Evolving Nature of Tech Job Interviews

2.1. **The Evolving Nature of Tech Job Interviews:** Tech job interviews have adapted to the digital age.

2.2. **Behavioural Interviews:** Behavioural questions assess your soft skills, problem-solving abilities, and teamwork.

2.3. **Technical Assessments:** Coding challenges and technical tests are common in tech job interviews.

2.4. **Video and Remote Interviews:** Remote and video interviews are increasingly common, requiring candidates to adapt to virtual settings.

3. Preparing for Technical Interviews

3.1. **Preparing for Technical Interviews:** Technical interviews can be challenging, so thorough preparation is essential.

3.2. **Coding Practice:** Practice coding problems and algorithms, and familiarize yourself with whiteboard or online coding platforms.

3.3. **System Design Interviews:** Be prepared to discuss the design of complex systems, architectures, and solutions.

3.4. **Behavioural and Soft Skills:** Develop concise and compelling responses to behavioural questions that showcase your problem-solving and teamwork skills.

4. Behavioural Interviews and Soft Skills

4.1. **Behavioural interviews and soft skills:** soft skills are equally important in tech interviews.

4.2. **Communication:** Effective communication is crucial for explaining your thought process and solutions clearly.

4.3. **Problem-Solving:** Demonstrate your problem-solving abilities by walking through real-world scenarios and challenges.

4.4. **Collaboration:** Highlight instances where you've worked effectively in teams and collaborated on projects.

5. Video and Remote Interviews

5.1. **Video and Remote Interviews:** Navigating virtual interviews requires specific considerations.

5.2. **Setup and Environment:** Ensure your video setup and background are professional and free from distractions.

5.3. **Practice:** Familiarize yourself with the video conferencing platform and practice with a friend or family member.

5.4. **Non-Verbal Communication:** Pay attention to your body language and maintain eye contact with the camera.

6. Post-Interview Follow-Up

6.1. **Post-Interview Follow-Up:** Following up after an interview can leave a positive impression.

6.2. **Thank-You Notes:** Send personalized thank-you notes to interviewers expressing your appreciation for the opportunity.

6.3. **Continuing Interest:** Reiterate your interest in the role and company, and inquire about the next steps in the hiring process.

6.4. **Professionalism:** Maintain professionalism in all your interactions, even after the interview.

Navigating tech job interviews and crafting an effective tech resume can be a challenging process, but it's crucial for securing your dream job in the tech industry. By tailoring your resume, preparing thoroughly for interviews, and adapting to the evolving nature of tech job interviews, you can increase your chances of success in this competitive field.

BALANCING WORK AND LIFE IN A TECH-DRIVEN WORLD

In a tech-driven world, maintaining a healthy work-life balance is crucial for overall well-being and sustained professional success. This section explores the challenges and strategies for achieving balance, addressing the impact of technology on work-life integration, and offering tips for a more harmonious life in the digital age.

1. The Challenge of Work-Life Balance in a Tech-Driven World

1.1. **The Challenge of Work-Life Balance:** Technology has blurred the boundaries between work and personal life.

1.2. **Digital Overload:** The constant connectivity of smartphones and email can lead to digital overload.

1.3. **Remote Work:** Remote work has made it challenging to separate work and personal spaces.

1.4. **Expectations and Pressure:** The expectation of immediate responses and the pressure to always be available can be overwhelming.

2. The Importance of Work-Life Balance

2.1. **The Importance of Work-Life Balance:** Maintaining a healthy balance is essential for well-being and productivity.

2.2. **Mental and Physical Health:** An imbalance can lead to stress, burnout, and adverse health effects.

2.3. **Productivity:** A well-balanced life often leads to increased productivity and job satisfaction.

2.4. **Sustainable Success:** Achieving long-term success requires a sustainable approach to work and life.

3. Strategies for Achieving Work-Life Balance

3.1. **Strategies for Achieving Work-Life Balance:** Several strategies can help restore equilibrium in a tech-driven world.

3.2. **Setting Boundaries:** Establish clear boundaries between work and personal time, and communicate them to colleagues and employers.

3.3. **Time Management:** Efficient time management techniques, such as the Pomodoro Technique, can boost productivity.

3.4. **Disconnecting:** Regularly disconnect from devices and work-related communication to recharge.

4. The Impact of Technology on Work-Life Integration

4.1. **The Impact of Technology:** Technology can both hinder and facilitate work-life integration.

4.2. **Flexibility:** Technology offers the flexibility to work from anywhere, allowing for a better blend of work and personal life.

4.3. **Digital Distractions:** On the other hand, it can be a source of constant distractions and intrusions into personal time.

4.4. **Digital Detox**: Practicing digital detox by unplugging for periods of time can help maintain balance.

5. Tips for a Harmonious Life in the Digital Age

5.1. **Tips for a Harmonious Life:** Practical tips for achieving a work-life balance in the digital age.

5.2. **Prioritize Self-Care:** Prioritize self-care, including exercise, relaxation, and hobbies.

5.3. **Regular Breaks:** Take regular breaks during work to recharge and refocus.

5.4. **Communication:** Open communication with employers and colleagues about your boundaries and expectations.

6. Rethinking Productivity and Success

6.1. **Rethinking Productivity and Success:** Shifting the focus from hours worked to results achieved.

6.2. **Output Over Hours:** Evaluate your productivity based on the quality of your output, not the number of hours you work.

6.3. **Defining Success:** Redefine success by including personal well-being and fulfillment in your definition.

6.4. **Continuous Adaptation:** Be willing to adapt and refine your work-life balance strategies as your circumstances change.

Maintaining a healthy work-life balance in a tech-driven world is essential for well-being and professional success. By setting boundaries, managing your time effectively, and embracing a flexible and adaptable approach, you can achieve a harmonious and fulfilling life in the digital age.

MENTORSHIP AND COMMUNITY: FINDING SUPPORT IN TECH

Navigating the tech industry can be more manageable and rewarding with the guidance of mentors and the support of a community. In this section, we'll explore the importance of mentorship and the benefits of being part of a tech community. We'll also offer insights into how to find mentors and engage with like-minded peers in the field.

1. The Value of Mentorship in Tech

1.1. **The Value of Mentorship:** Mentorship is a valuable resource for personal and professional growth in the tech industry.

1.2. **Guidance and Advice:** Mentors provide guidance, advice, and insights based on their experience.

1.3. **Skill Development:** They help you develop your skills, set goals, and navigate career challenges.

1.4. **Networking Opportunities:** Mentors introduce you to valuable connections within the tech industry.

2. Finding a Tech Mentor

2.1. **Finding a Tech Mentor:** Identifying and connecting with a suitable mentor is a key step.

2.2. **Identify Your Needs:** Determine what you're seeking in a mentor, whether it's career advice, technical guidance, or leadership development.

2.3. **Professional Networks:** Attend industry events, join tech organizations, and engage with online communities to meet potential mentors.

2.4. **Ask for Mentorship:** Approach potential mentors respectfully and express your desire to learn from their experience.

3. Engaging with a Tech Community

3.1. **Engaging with a Tech Community:** Being part of a tech community provides support and opportunities for growth.

3.2. **Online Forums:** Participate in online forums, tech communities, and social media groups related to your field of interest.

3.3. **Local Meetups and Conferences:** Attend local tech meetups, conferences, and networking events to connect with like-minded professionals.

3.4. **Open Source Projects:** Contribute to open source projects to collaborate with others and showcase your skills.

4. Benefits of a Tech Community

4.1. **Benefits of a Tech Community:** Tech communities offer numerous advantages.

4.2. **Knowledge Sharing:** Communities foster knowledge sharing, helping members stay up to date with industry trends.

4.3. **Collaboration Opportunities:** You can find opportunities for collaboration and potential job leads within a community.

4.4. **Support and Encouragement:** Tech communities provide support, encouragement, and a sense of belonging.

5. Mentoring Others and Giving Back

5.1. **Mentoring Others and Giving Back:** As you progress in your tech career, consider becoming a mentor to others.

5.2. **Pay It Forward:** Sharing your knowledge and experience can be incredibly rewarding and a way to give back.

5.3. **Professional Growth:** Mentoring others can also help you reinforce your own understanding and skills.

5.4. **Community Building:** Contributing to a tech community by mentoring strengthens the community as a whole.

6. Making the Most of Mentorship and Community

6.1. **Making the Most of Mentorship and Community:** To maximize the benefits of mentorship and community involvement:

6.2. **Set Clear Goals:** Clearly define your goals and expectations from mentorship and community engagement.

6.3. **Be Proactive:** Take the initiative to seek advice and opportunities within the community.

6.4. **Show Gratitude:** Express your gratitude to mentors and the community for their support and guidance.

Mentorship and community involvement are cornerstones of success in the tech industry. Embracing these relationships and being an active part of the tech community can accelerate your growth, provide you with invaluable guidance, and open doors to opportunities you might not have found otherwise.

STAYING ETHICAL AND RESPONSIBLE IN TECH CAREERS

In a rapidly evolving tech landscape, maintaining ethics and responsibility is paramount. This section explores the ethical challenges in tech careers, offers guidance on making responsible decisions, and emphasizes the importance of ethical leadership in the digital age.

1. The Ethical Landscape of Tech

1.1. **The Ethical Landscape of Tech:** Tech careers often encounter ethical dilemmas in various areas.

1.2. **Privacy:** Issues surrounding data privacy, surveillance, and the responsible use of personal information.

1.3. **Artificial Intelligence:** Ethical considerations in AI, including bias, transparency, and accountability.

1.4. **Cybersecurity:** Balancing security with responsible disclosure and protecting against malicious uses of technology.

2. Ethical Decision-Making

2.1. **Ethical Decision-Making:** Developing a framework for making ethical decisions is essential.

2.2. **Ethical Guidelines:** Familiarize yourself with industry-specific ethical guidelines, such as those from ACM or IEEE.

2.3. **Stakeholder Consideration:** Assess the impact of decisions on various stakeholders, including customers, employees, and society.

2.4. **Balancing Interests:** Consider the balance between business goals and ethical responsibility.

3. Responsible AI and Data Use

3.1. **Responsible AI and Data Use:** In the age of AI, it's vital to act responsibly with data and algorithms.

3.2. **Data Ethics:** Implement data ethics by respecting data privacy and ensuring informed consent.

3.3. **Algorithmic Transparency:** Strive for transparency in AI systems and disclose their decision-making processes.

3.4. **Accountability:** Establish clear lines of accountability for AI systems and their outcomes.

4. **Leadership and Ethical Culture**

   4.1. **Leadership and Ethical Culture:** Ethical leadership sets the tone for responsible decision-making within a tech organization.

   4.2. **Leading by Example:** Leaders should exemplify ethical behavior and foster a culture of responsibility.

   4.3. **Communication:** Promote open and honest communication about ethical issues within the organization.

   4.4. **Ethical Training:** Provide ethical training and resources to employees to enhance their understanding.

5. **Addressing Bias and Inclusion**

   5.1. **Addressing Bias and Inclusion:** Tackling biases and promoting diversity and inclusion are ethical imperatives.

   5.2. **Bias Mitigation:** Take steps to mitigate biases in AI systems and algorithms, ensuring fairness.

   5.3. **Inclusive Practices:** Embrace inclusive hiring, promote diversity, and foster an inclusive work environment.

5.4. **User-Centric Design:** Prioritize user-cantered design to create products that serve diverse user needs.

6. Ethical Responsibility in Innovation

6.1. **Ethical Responsibility in Innovation:** Innovations should align with ethical considerations.

6.2. **Risk Assessment:** Evaluate the ethical risks and potential consequences of new technologies.

6.3. **Ethical Testing:** Rigorous ethical testing should be part of the development process.

6.4. **Regulation and Compliance:** Comply with relevant regulations and advocate for ethical regulation when needed.

7. Reporting and Whistleblowing

7.1. **Reporting and Whistleblowing:** Encourage a culture of reporting and whistle-blower protection.

7.2. **Ethical Concern Reporting:** Establish clear processes for employees to report ethical concerns.

7.3. **Whistle-blower Protection:** Ensure that whistle-blowers are protected from retaliation.

7.4. **Ethical Investigation:** Investigate reported concerns thoroughly and transparently.

8. **Accountability and Learning from Mistakes**

8.1. **Accountability and Learning from Mistakes:** Acknowledge and learn from ethical mistakes.

8.2. **Accountability Measures:** Implement accountability measures when ethical breaches occur.

8.3. **Continuous Learning:** Use ethical lapses as opportunities for continuous improvement and learning.

8.4. **Transparency:** Be transparent about mistakes and the actions taken to address them.

Staying ethical and responsible in tech careers is not only a moral imperative but also essential for the long-term success and sustainability of tech organizations. By adhering to ethical principles, making responsible decisions, and fostering an ethical culture, tech professionals can contribute to a more responsible and ethical tech industry.

THE FUTURE OF WORK: PREDICTIONS AND TRENDS

As technology continues to transform industries and reshape the workforce, it's crucial to understand the future of work. In this section, we'll explore predictions and trends that are likely to define the future of work in the tech-driven world, providing insights into the evolving landscape of employment and career opportunities.

1. **The Rise of Remote and Hybrid Work**

   1.1. **The Rise of Remote and Hybrid Work:** Remote work, which saw a significant boost during global events, is expected to become a permanent fixture.

   1.2. **Flexible Work Arrangements:** Employees will continue to seek flexible work arrangements that accommodate remote and in-person work.

   1.3. **Virtual Teams:** Organizations will rely on virtual teams and remote collaboration tools for global reach.

   1.4. **Work-Life Integration:** A focus on work-life integration will replace the traditional work-life balance.

2. Automation and Augmentation of Jobs

2.1. **Automation and Augmentation of Jobs:** Automation will change the nature of work, with jobs being augmented rather than replaced.

2.2. **Collaborative Robots:** Cobots will work alongside humans, particularly in manufacturing and logistics.

2.3. **AI Enhancements:** AI will enhance decision-making and problem-solving in various fields, from medicine to finance.

2.4. **Upskilling and Reskilling:** The need for continuous learning and adaptation will be more critical than ever.

3. Gig Economy and Freelancing

3.1. **Gig Economy and Freelancing:** The gig economy will continue to grow, offering diverse opportunities for independent workers.

3.2. **Freelance Platforms:** Online platforms will connect freelancers with employers, making it easier to find project-based work.

3.3. **Skills Marketplace:** The emphasis will shift from traditional job titles to skills, enabling gig workers to offer their expertise in various contexts.

3.4. **Income Diversification**: Many individuals will pursue income diversification through a mix of gig work and part-time jobs.

4. Artificial Intelligence in Recruitment

4.1. **Artificial Intelligence in Recruitment:** AI will play a significant role in the hiring process.

4.2. **Automated Screening:** AI will automate the initial screening of candidates, saving time for recruiters.

4.3. **Bias Mitigation:** AI will help reduce bias in hiring decisions by focusing on objective criteria.

4.4. **Skills-Based Hiring:** Hiring will increasingly be based on skills and competencies rather than traditional qualifications.

5. Emphasis on Soft Skills

5.1. **Emphasis on Soft Skills:** Soft skills will become increasingly important in the tech-driven job market.

5.2. **Communication and Collaboration:** Effective communication and collaboration will be crucial for remote and virtual teams.

5.3. **Emotional Intelligence:** Understanding and managing emotions will enhance teamwork and leadership.

5.4. **Adaptability:** The ability to adapt to change and learn new skills will be highly valued.

6. Sustainability and Purpose-Driven Work

6.1. **Sustainability and Purpose-Driven Work:** Employees will seek work that aligns with their values and societal impact.

6.2. **Corporate Responsibility:** Companies will place greater emphasis on social and environmental responsibility.

6.3. **Sustainable Practices:** The adoption of sustainable practices will become standard across industries.

6.4. **Impact-Driven Careers:** More individuals will choose careers that make a positive impact on society.

7. Lifelong Learning as a Necessity

7.1. Lifelong Learning as a Necessity: The need for continuous learning and skill development will be a career-long endeavour.

7.2. Continuous Reskilling: Individuals will regularly reskill to adapt to changing job requirements.

7.3. Microlearning: Short, focused learning modules will facilitate just-in-time skill acquisition.

7.4. Online Education: Online platforms will be primary sources for ongoing education and professional development.

The future of work is a dynamic landscape shaped by technology, societal changes, and individual aspirations. By staying informed about emerging trends, embracing lifelong learning, and being adaptable, individuals can position themselves for success in a rapidly evolving job market.

RESOURCES FOR STAYING INFORMED AND UPDATED

In the ever-evolving world of tech and the digital age, staying informed and updated is essential for personal and professional growth. This section provides a comprehensive list of resources that tech professionals can tap into to remain current and relevant in their fields.

1. Online Learning Platforms

1.1. **Coursera:** Offers a wide range of online courses from top universities and institutions on various tech-related subjects.

1.2. **edX:** Provides free and paid online courses, including micro degrees, in collaboration with universities and organizations.

1.3. **LinkedIn Learning:** Offers video courses on tech and business topics, including software development, data science, and more.

2. Tech News and Blogs

2.1. **TechCrunch:** A leading source for tech news, start-up stories, and product launches.

2.2. **Wired:** Covers tech, business, and science, exploring the impact of technology on society.

2.3. **Mashable:** Features news and reviews on tech, digital culture, and entertainment.

3. Industry Publications and Journals

3.1. **MIT Technology Review:** Provides in-depth analysis of emerging technologies and their impact on business and society.

3.2. **IEEE Spectrum:** Covers a wide range of tech topics, including emerging trends in engineering, computing, and telecommunications.

3.3. **Harvard Business Review:** Offers articles on tech leadership, innovation, and digital transformation in business.

4. Podcasts

4.1. **"Reply All":** A podcast about the internet and digital culture, exploring intriguing tech-related stories.

4.2. **"The Verge cast":** Weekly tech discussions covering the latest in consumer technology and tech culture.

4.3. **"Startups"**: Offers a behind-the-scenes look at what it's really like to start and run a business.

5. Professional Organizations

5.1. **Association for Computing Machinery (ACM):** A global organization that provides resources and support for computing professionals.

5.2. **Institute of Electrical and Electronics Engineers (IEEE)**: Focuses on electrical and electronics engineering and offers resources for tech professionals.

5.3. **Project Management Institute (PMI):** Supports project managers and provides resources for project management professionals.

6. Online Communities and Forums

6.1. **Stack Overflow:** A community-driven Q&A platform where tech professionals can ask questions and share knowledge.

6.2. **GitHub:** A platform for collaborating on software development projects and learning from others' code.

6.3. **Tech-related Subreddits:** Subreddits such as r/programming, r/data science, and r/webdev offer discussions and insights.

7. Tech Conferences and Webinars

7.1. **Google I/O:** Google's annual developer conference, where they announce new technologies and platforms.

7.2. **Apple WWDC:** Apple's Worldwide Developers Conference for the latest on iOS, macOS, and more.

7.3. **Microsoft Ignite:** Microsoft's conference for tech professionals to learn about the latest in Microsoft technologies.

8. Online Courses and Tutorials

8.1. **Udacity:** Offers tech-focused online courses and nanodegrees in fields like AI, programming, and data science.

8.2. **Codecademy:** Provides interactive coding lessons and projects to help learners build practical skills.

8.3. **Khan Academy:** Offers free online courses on a variety of subjects, including computer science and programming.

9. Online Publications for Specific Tech Fields

9.1. Smashing Magazine: A resource for web designers and developers, with articles, tutorials, and industry insights.

9.2. Towards Data Science (Medium): Focuses on data science and machine learning with articles and tutorials.

9.3. Dev.to: A platform for developers to share articles, tips, and insights on coding and development.

10. Social Media and Tech Influencers

X: Follow tech influencers, industry experts, and organizations to stay updated on the latest trends.

YouTube: Subscribe to tech channels that offer tutorials, reviews, and discussions on various tech topics.

LinkedIn: Connect with professionals and join relevant tech groups to access industry updates and discussions.

Staying informed and updated is an ongoing commitment, but the wealth of resources available to tech professionals makes it easier than ever to stay current and relevant in a rapidly changing industry. These resources encompass a wide range of formats and platforms, allowing individuals to choose the methods that best suit their learning preferences and career goals.

CONCLUSION: YOUR JOURNEY TO A FUTURE-READY TECH CAREER

In this dynamic and ever-changing world of technology, your journey to a future-ready tech career has been nothing short of extraordinary. You've explored the shifting landscape of tech careers, witnessed the profound impact of automation, and navigated the challenges and ethical considerations that come with it. You've also embraced the transformative power of AI, cloud computing, and blockchain, and have delved into the promising world of web3 and biometric security. As you've discovered, the opportunities in the tech industry are limitless, but they also come with the responsibility of continuous learning, adaptability, and ethical decision-making.

Your path to success in the tech industry is not just about the hard skills you acquire or the specific technologies you master. It's about developing a growth mindset, embracing change, and building a personal brand that reflects your unique strengths and values. You've learned how to craft a tech resume that shines and how to shine in tech job interviews, whether in person or on a virtual screen.

You've explored the ethical challenges that come with the power of technology and discovered the importance of responsible decision-making and leadership.

You understand the significance of addressing bias, promoting diversity and inclusion, and ensuring that your innovations are not only groundbreaking but also ethical and sustainable.

The future of work, as you've learned, is a landscape of remote and hybrid work, AI augmentation, the gig economy, and a growing emphasis on soft skills, sustainability, and lifelong learning. You've seen that the future belongs to those who can adapt, learn, and embrace change with enthusiasm.

Moreover, you've discovered the importance of mentorship and community. The guidance of mentors and the support of a tech community can be your compass in this ever-evolving world. You've learned how to find mentors, engage with tech communities, and contribute to the growth of both yourself and the tech industry.

Finally, you've explored a wealth of resources to stay informed and updated, from online courses and tech news to professional organizations and online communities. In this digital age, access to knowledge is abundant, and the tools you need to succeed are at your fingertips.

Your journey to a future-ready tech career is ongoing. Technology will continue to advance, industries will evolve, and new opportunities will emerge. The key to your success lies in your adaptability, your commitment to continuous learning, and your dedication to ethical and responsible practices.

As you move forward in your tech career, remember that you are not alone on this journey. The tech community is vast, diverse, and eager to support you. Mentorship is within reach, and the resources to fuel your growth are abundant. Your future-ready tech career is not just a destination but a lifelong adventure filled with learning, innovation, and the chance to make a positive impact on the world.

With the knowledge and insights, you've gained, you are well-equipped to embrace the challenges and opportunities of the tech industry. Your journey is now, and your future is ready.

GLOSSARY

1. **Artificial Intelligence (AI):** AI refers to the simulation of human intelligence in machines that are programmed to think, learn, and problem-solve like humans. It includes tasks such as natural language processing, speech recognition, and image recognition.

2. **Blockchain:** A decentralized and distributed digital ledger technology used to record transactions across multiple computers. It's best known for its application in cryptocurrencies like Bitcoin.

3. **Cloud Computing:** The delivery of computing services, including storage, servers, databases, networking, software, analytics, and more, over the internet (the "cloud"). This technology eliminates the need for on-premises infrastructure.

4. **Cryptocurrency:** Digital or virtual currencies that use cryptography for security. The most well-known cryptocurrency is Bitcoin, but there are many others like Ethereum, Litecoin, and Ripple.

5. **Big Data:** Extremely large datasets that may be analysed computationally to reveal patterns, trends, and associations, especially relating to human behavior and interactions.

6. **Internet of Things (IoT):** The network of interconnected physical objects (devices) that communicate and exchange data with each other over the internet, often for monitoring or control purposes.

7. **Machine Learning:** A subset of AI that focuses on the development of algorithms and statistical models that computer systems can use to perform specific tasks without explicit programming.

8. **Cybersecurity:** The practice of protecting computer systems, networks, and data from theft, damage, or unauthorized access. It involves various technologies and processes.

9. **Data Science:** An interdisciplinary field that uses scientific methods, algorithms, processes, and systems to extract knowledge and insights from structured and unstructured data.

10. **Biometric Security:** Security measures that use physical or behavioural characteristics, such as fingerprints, facial recognition, or voice recognition, to authenticate users.

11. **Web3:** An emerging paradigm for the internet that focuses on decentralization and blockchain technology. It aims to give users more control over their data and digital identities.

12. **Virtual Reality (VR):** A technology that immerses users in a computer-generated environment, typically experienced through a headset.

13. **Augmented Reality (AR):** Technology that overlays digital information, such as images and sound, on the real world, often through the use of a smartphone or AR glasses.

14. **Deep Learning:** A subfield of machine learning that involves neural networks with multiple layers, allowing the model to automatically learn and make decisions without human intervention.

15. **DevOps:** A set of practices that combines software development (Dev) and IT operations (Ops) to reduce the systems development life cycle and provide continuous delivery.

16. **User Experience (UX) Design:** The process of enhancing user satisfaction with a product by improving the usability, accessibility, and pleasure provided in the interaction with it.

17. **User Interface (UI) Design:** The design of the graphical layout and elements of a digital product, such as a website or mobile app, with a focus on aesthetics and usability.

18. **Data Scientist:** A professional who analyses and interprets complex data to help organizations make data-driven decisions.

19. **Cybersecurity Expert:** A professional who specializes in protecting an organization's information systems and data from cyber threats and attacks.

20. **EdTech:** Educational technology, which includes digital tools, platforms, and software used to enhance and support learning and teaching.

21. **Gig Economy:** A labour market characterized by short-term contracts and freelance work, where individuals are hired for specific projects or tasks rather than traditional full-time employment.

22. **Telemedicine:** The practice of providing remote medical care and consultations through telecommunication technology, allowing patients and healthcare providers to connect virtually.

23. **Smart Cities:** Urban areas that use technology and data to improve efficiency, sustainability, and the overall quality of life for their residents. This may include initiatives like smart transportation and energy management.

24. **Legal Tech:** The use of technology, such as software and AI, to streamline and improve the practice of law and the delivery of legal services.

25. **EdTech:** Educational technology, which includes digital tools, platforms, and software used to enhance and support learning and teaching.

26. **Sustainability:** The practice of reducing negative environmental impacts through responsible resource use and consideration for future generations.

27. **Biometrics:** The measurement and statistical analysis of people's unique physical and behavioural characteristics, such as fingerprints, facial recognition, and voice patterns.

28. **Open Source:** Software or projects that have publicly available source code and are developed and maintained by a community of volunteers, allowing anyone to view, use, or contribute to the code.

29. **Hackathon:** An event where programmers, designers, and other tech enthusiasts collaborate intensively on software projects, often within a limited timeframe.

30. **Machine Vision:** Technology that allows machines, such as computers or robots, to interpret and understand visual information from the world, similar to human vision.

31. **API (Application Programming Interface):** A set of rules and protocols that allow different software applications to communicate with each other and share data or functionality.

32. **AR/VR Development:** The process of creating augmented reality (AR) and virtual reality (VR) applications and experiences, often involving 3D modelling, spatial tracking, and immersive interaction.

33. **Cyber Threats:** Various forms of security risks that can compromise computer systems, networks, and data, including malware, phishing, and hacking.

34. Disruptive Technology: Innovations or technologies that significantly alter or revolutionize industries, often by displacing established market leaders.

35. **Agile Methodology:** A project management approach that emphasizes flexibility and collaboration in software development and other projects, allowing teams to adapt to changing requirements.

36. **Start-up:** A newly founded business or company that is often characterized by innovation, rapid growth, and a focus on scaling quickly.

37. **IoT Devices:** Physical objects or gadgets that are connected to the internet and can collect and transmit data, such as smart thermostats, fitness trackers, and connected appliances.

38. **AI Ethics:** The ethical considerations and principles surrounding the use of artificial intelligence, including transparency, accountability, and fairness.

~~~~~~~~~~~~~~~~~~~~~**END**~~~~~~~~~~~~~~~~~~~~~

www.ingramcontent.com/pod-product-compliance
Lightning Source LLC
Chambersburg PA
CBHW051236050326
40689CB00007B/939